Sea Cows, Shamans, and Scurvy

Alaska's First Naturalist:
Georg Wilhelm Steller

ALSO BY ANN ARNOLD

The Adventurous Chef: Alexis Soyer

SEA COWS, SHAMANS, AND SCURVY

ALASKA'S FIRST NATURALIST:
GEORG WILHELM STELLER

ANN ARNOLD

SIBERIA
ARCTIC SEAS
Sea of Okhotsk
KAMCHATKA
ALASKA
BERING SEA

FRANCES FOSTER BOOKS
FARRAR STRAUS GIROUX

NEW YORK

Permissions acknowledgments appear on page ix.

www.fsgkidsbooks.com

Library of Congress Cataloging-in-Publication Data
Arnold, Ann.
   Sea cows, shamans, and scurvy : Alaska's first naturalist : Georg Wilhelm
Steller / Ann Arnold.— 1st ed.
      p.   cm.
   Includes bibliographical references and index.
   ISBN-13: 978-0-374-39947-4
   ISBN-10: 0-374-39947-6
   1. Steller, Georg Wilhelm, 1709–1746.   2. Explorers—Alaska—Biography.
3. Explorers—Russia (Federation)—Russian Far East—Biography.
4. Naturalists—Alaska—Biography.   I. Title.

G226.S8A76 2008
508.092—dc22
[B]

                                                    2006037400

For Mara, Margritt, and Wieland

ACKNOWLEDGMENTS

I would like to thank both the willing and the unwilling contributors to this biography. Professor Margritt Engel, professor emerita at the University of Alaska, Anchorage, delighted me with tales of modern Russian scholarship, German superstition, and the less scientific side of Georg Steller's personality. Carol Urness, professor emerita at the University of Minnesota, Minneapolis, patiently explained the purposes of the Kamchatka expeditions and convinced me of Bering's successful leadership of the first. Anthony Arnold translated Russian articles for me and drew comparisons between eighteenth- and twentieth-century political life in Russia. Professor Kenneth J. Carpenter kindly reviewed my note about scurvy and made suggestions that I have incorporated. Mara Luckmann translated German writings for me, as did Margritt Engel and Harry Wohlmuth.

Rudolf Schmid, professor emeritus of botany in the Department of Integrative Biology at the University of California, Berkeley, and book review editor of *Taxon: International Journal of Plant Taxonomy, Phylogeny and Evolution*, contributed the concordance of common names and their scientific equivalents. Both he and the naturalist Percy Mussells have allowed me to borrow volumes from their libraries to help with the illustrations.

My editor, Frances Foster, encouraged me to persevere as this book grew from a forty-page picture book to a much longer book for young adults. She and the designer, Barbara Grzeslo, with their flexibility, imagination, and organizing vision have molded my ungainly heap of manuscript, with its floodplain of illustrations, into what you see before you. Their support has reminded me of my son's words "Remember Shackleton!" as we trudged, baggage-laden, through the rain on a busless Sunday to a remote Italian railway station. I hope that youthful readers may someday give heart to their own parents with "Remember Steller!"

Lydia T. Black, professor emerita at the University of Alaska, Fairbanks, was kind enough to speak to me about her research and opinions. Richard Dauenhauer, President's Professor of Alaskan Native Languages at the University of Alaska Southeast in Juneau, gave me information about Chirikov's landing site and the words spoken by the native boatmen.

I am grateful to Professor Peter Ulf Møller of the Slavic Department at the University of Aarhus in Denmark, who answered my dozens of questions. His extensive knowledge of the naval part of the expedition enabled me to include anecdotal information from his research, such as the fact that Anna Bering and her children traveled from Okhotsk in sedan chairs.

Michael Schlosser gave me every possible assistance during my stay in Bad Windsheim, spending several hours showing me volumes Steller could have seen in the municipal library (established in 1559), and making special arrangements at the local folk museum that allowed me to draw a bedroom similar to that in which Steller was born.

Dr. Wieland Hintzsche, historian of science at the Francke Foundations in Halle, Germany, has read my text twice, questioning and correcting my assumptions, conclusions, and facts in the light of his long and deep acquaintance with Steller's manuscripts. He and his wife, Dr. Elisabeth Hintzsche, shared their home and extended their hospitality to me when I visited Halle for the conference on collecting in Siberia held under the auspices of the Max Planck Institute. There they announced their plans for establishing the International Georg Wilhelm Steller Society to celebrate the three hundredth anniversary of Steller's birth. I am very grateful to them both.

To my husband, Ian Jackson, I owe the deepest debt of gratitude. After we attended an exhibition at the California Academy of Sciences concerning Russian exploration of America, he answered my first question—"Who was Georg Steller?"—by handing me Leonhard Stejneger's biography from his beautifully ordered shelves. As my queries increased he found volume upon volume to satisfy my curiosity and help me try to bring the project to completion.

ACKNOWLEDGMENTS TO PUBLISHERS

Grateful acknowledgment is made for permission to reprint material from the following publications:

Reprinted by permission of the publisher from *George Wilhelm Steller: The Pioneer of Alaskan Natural History* by Leonhard Stejneger, 44, 68, 70, 83, 97, 135, 145, 146, 147, 148, 163, 168, 169, 170, 171, 172, 390, 395, 418, 478, Cambridge, Mass.: Harvard University Press. Copyright © 1936 by the President and Fellows of Harvard College.

From George W. Steller / O. W. Frost (ed.) *Journal of a Voyage with Bering, 1741–1742.* Copyright © 1992 by the Board of Trustees of the Leland Stanford Jr. University.

Excerpts from F. A. Golder, *Bering's Voyages: An Account of the Efforts of the Russians to Determine the Relation of Asia and America.* Copyright © 1922 by American Geographical Society, New York, New York.

Excerpts from *Steller's History of Kamchatka: Collected Information Concerning the History of Kamchatka, Its Peoples, Their Manners, Names, Lifestyles, and Various Customary Practices.* English translation copyright © 2003 by the University of Alaska Press.

CONTENTS

Sea Cows, Shamans, and Scurvy

Alaska's First Naturalist:
Georg Wilhelm
Steller

I

Sonntagskind:
A Sunday's Child
1709–1734

I N ANCIENT GREECE AND ROME A CHILD BORN ON
Sunday was thought to be blessed with magical gifts
and good fortune. The Romans called him *albae gallinae
filius*, child of the white hen, or *fortunae filius*, fortune's
child.

In German-speaking countries he is called a *Sonntagskind*, and in their legends and fairy tales only a Sunday's child can make contact with the realm of the
spirits, be released from a spell, unearth treasures, have
dreams fulfilled, and bring good fortune to others.

A *Sonntagskind* is able to give the worst disaster a
happy outcome. Even today, in Austria and Germany,
people will say of someone whose luck quickly shifts
from bad to good, "He must be a *Sonntagskind*."

WINDSHEIM

O N SUNDAY, MARCH 10, 1709, IN THE LUTHERAN CITY OF
Windsheim, a dead baby was born to the Stöller family. The
midwife, having tried everything she knew to revive him, packed
her bag and departed. But the mother's sister, who was attending
the birth, would not give up hope for this *Sonntagskind*. The infant's
oldest brother, Augustin, watched as she wrapped the baby in hot
blankets, replacing them when they became cold. At last, to everyone's amazement, the baby gave a loud cry.

That afternoon he was christened Georg Wilhelm.

At the age of five, Georg entered the local Latin school, where
his father was the music teacher. Every subject was taught in Latin,
the language understood by learned people throughout Europe.

When he was fifteen, Georg won a scholarship to the highest

level of the school and was required
to sing in the church choir on special religious occasions. His other
duty was to clean the town library,
dusting the beautiful vellum-bound
atlases and books about medicinal
plants. He studied long hours and
was always first in his class.

On holidays he discovered his
love of nature in the nearby Schosz-
bach Forest, where gray herons nested and foxes, badgers, and river
otters made their homes. He became familiar with the many rare
and unusual plants that grew only in the region around Windsheim.

In 1729, when Georg was twenty years old, he received a scholarship to study religion and medicine at the University of Wittenberg. Everyone assumed he would return in a few years to become a
Lutheran minister in his native town. In fact, he never went back to
Windsheim and never saw his parents again.

After he completed his studies in Wittenberg, his scientific interests led him to the University of Halle, where he could study
natural history by enrolling as a medical student and continue his

religious education. He had no professor of botany or zoology as
such during his first year, but he learned anatomy through the dis-
section of animals, and botany from the study of medicinal plants.

However, Georg went far beyond the courses offered by the university. Guided by published floras of the area, he extended his botany lessons to the countryside around Halle.

In Georg's second year, the internationally famous anatomist and zoologist Johann Friedrich Cassebohm joined the faculty as professor of medicine. Georg immediately enrolled in his zoology classes, where he was taught about animal development. The microscope introduced him to a new world of minute organisms.

During his vacations Georg took walking trips to visit his brother Augustin, who was practicing medicine twenty miles away, in Köthen. On one occasion he walked in the Harz Mountains, where he was awestruck by the dizzying depths of the cavernous Stolberg mines.

Georg paid for his medical training and earned his room and board by teaching classes and supervising a boys' dormitory in the Latin school of the famous Francke Foundations, an institution that began as an orphanage and soon grew to encompass a whole village of schools. He became friendly with the oldest boy, Elias Reichard, who had returned to prepare for university after working for several years as a linen weaver's apprentice. Elias received special permission to stay up later than the other students so that Georg could help him with difficult subjects. The record of their friendship offers evidence of a prophetic side to Georg's character, one aspect of a *Sonntagskind*.

Many years later, Elias recounted a conversation they had one night by the fireside while talking about supernatural experiences. When Georg claimed that he could see into the future, Elias begged him to do so. Georg began, "I am shortly going to fall into a serious illness (during which you, my dear Reichard, are going to sit up with me several nights), from which, however, I will recover, leave Halle, travel to the extreme end of Europe, suffer shipwreck, be cast upon an uninhabited island and die in a distant country."

Elias then held out his hand and asked his own fate. Georg scrutinized the lines on Elias's palm and answered, "You will unexpectedly make the acquaintance of my oldest brother [Augustin]; however backward you still are in your studies, in  the course of eight or nine years you will obtain a professorship . . . A short time later you will lose your father by death and only see him in his coffin; you will marry two noble ladies in succession and will reach the age of about eighty years."

Soon after this conversation the first prediction came true when Georg contracted a violent fever. Elias sat up with him for three nights, nursing him back to health.

In the following years the future unfolded just as Georg had foretold.

The Francke Foundations had a remarkable Cabinet of Artifacts and Curiosities, a collection of several thousand natural and man-made objects from around the world, used for teaching the students. Among its treasures were a crocodile, a swordfish, the horn of a narwhal, and a stuffed lizard three and a half feet long. Lutheran missionaries had sent quantities of seashells from the Indian Ocean and cases of preserved insects from Malabar, in India. As Georg and Professor Cassebohm explored this accumulation of preserved exotic creatures and anthropological artifacts brought back by travelers and former students, Georg may well have longed to explore far-away places himself and return with plants and animals no one in Halle had ever seen.

He discussed the possibility of going to Russia with his professors. In Germany there were too few university positions for the growing number of educated men, while the Russian capital of St. Petersburg, with its newly formed Imperial Academy of Sciences, offered many opportunities. A few years before, the brilliant Dr. Johann Georg Gmelin from Tübingen, who had earned his doctorate when he was only nineteen years old, had passed through Halle on his way to St. Petersburg. In just three years he had become a professor at the Academy. Now Professor Gmelin, no older than Georg Stöller, was preparing to embark on the Second Kamchatka Expedition.

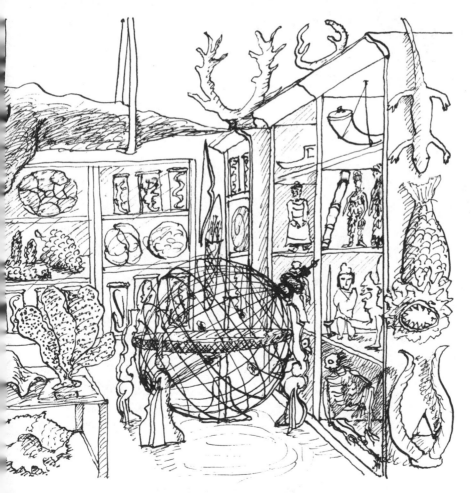

2

Russia's Great Explorations:
The First and Second
Kamchatka Expeditions
1725-1730 AND 1733-1743

KINGDOM of SWEDEN

Baltic Sea

St. Petersburg

Moscow

Kazan

Volga River

URAL MTS.

Tobolsk

Tura R.

Ob River

THE SECOND KAMCHATKA EXPEDITION WAS RUSSIA'S AT-
tempt to explore, describe, and map its vast lands from the
Ural Mountains across Siberia to Kamchatka and, if possible, lay
claim to the northwest coast of America—if the sailors could find
it, for no European had ever reached America by this route.

It had started simply enough. In 1725, Peter the Great, Czar of
Russia, had ordered Vitus Jonassen Bering, a Dane who had been
made a captain in the Russian Navy after the recently concluded
war with Sweden, to travel across Siberia, mapping the thousands
of miles from Tobolsk to the settlement of Okhotsk on the eastern-
most shores of Siberia. There he was to build a ship, the *Fortuna*, in
which to carry workers and materials for a second ship across the

Sea of Okhotsk to the Kamchatka Peninsula. A second ship, the *St. Gabriel*, would be built at the mouth of the Kamchatka River on the eastern coast of the peninsula. Captain Bering was ordered to chart the northeast coast of Kamchatka in the *St. Gabriel*, determining whether Russia and America were connected by land. He was then to return to St. Petersburg with his maps and his findings. Czar Peter died four days before Bering's departure, so the Czar's widow, Catherine I, handed Bering his sailing orders.

Bering returned five years later to a new ruler, Empress Anna, and the members of the recently formed Academy of Sciences, who were not convinced by his claim that Russia and America lay on separate continents. These armchair scholars complained that he had not sailed far enough north and he should not have returned so

hastily. Bering patiently explained his caution: soon the winter ice would be forming in the sea north of Kamchatka; his ship did not have enough provisions to overwinter in an ice-locked sea; shorter autumn days and foggy or stormy weather made shipwrecks more likely. Besides, his mission had been successful, and he had beautiful new maps to prove it. As his ship sailed north along the coast of Kamchatka, Bering had sighted floating trees of a size and kind unknown on the Kamchatka Peninsula; a different landmass must be nearby. Bering offered to lead another mapping expedition to seek ocean trade routes to Japan and to find the land that he believed lay on a separate continent to the east of Kamchatka. The Second Kamchatka Expedition grew out of his proposal.

Two years passed while the Admiralty, the Academy of Sciences, and the Russian Administrative Senate added further objectives to the plan. The trials of the First Kamchatka Expedition almost defeated the stamina and resourcefulness of Vitus Bering; the Second was to be an even greater challenge. Bering's responsibilities were enormous—comparable to organizing an army of several divisions. Over a period of years he had to clothe, feed, and shelter hundreds —sometimes thousands—of people while transporting them across the vast, inhospitable land of Siberia, often with rivers as the only roadways. Not everyone traveled together. Time and means of movement were dictated by season, weather, and terrain. Often there were many days' journey between sources of food and shelter. Bering's men were plagued by insects during the brief summers and threatened by frostbite throughout the long snowy winters.

In addition to facing all the hardships of exploring Siberia, Bering had to deal tactfully with the prickly and demanding professors from the Academy of Sciences, the obstructive governors of Siberia, and the unimaginative senators resentfully supplying rubles from their comfortable palaces in St. Petersburg.

The Senate instructed Bering to build and provision ships for several separate mapping expeditions as he traveled the breadth of the Russian Empire. He was ordered to set in motion two parties of men: one, starting from Tobolsk, to chart the course of the Ob River and the other, starting from Yakutsk, to chart the Lena River. Both groups were instructed to travel north through Siberia to the seas bordering the Arctic Ocean. From there they were to map the Siberian coastline to Kamchatka and determine, once and for all, whether Siberia and America were one landmass. While these mapping expeditions were in progress, Bering was to go on to Yakutsk. There his men would mine and forge iron ore into everything from nails to cannonballs, construct sledges and riverboats, and gather provisions for his voyages to Kamchatka and America.

As leader of the expedition, Bering had many tasks to delegate. Fortunately, he could rely on Martin Spangberg and Aleksei Chirikov, the two experienced officers he had trained on the First Kamchatka Expedition. Before sailing on their own explorations, both captains were to play important roles in constructing ships and boats of all kinds and amassing building materials and food for everyone on the expedition. Bering's second-in-command, Captain Spangberg, was to travel with his own party to Okhotsk, where he would build ships and prepare for his charting expedition to the Kuril Islands and Japan. Then he would begin construction of vessels for Bering. Captain Aleksei Chirikov, the third-in-command, was to organize the provisioning of the remote outpost of Okhotsk. Ultimately he would be captain of his own ship, sailing alongside Bering to America.

The Academy had its own ambitions for the expedition. To lead the Academy contingent, it chose two of Georg's fellow countrymen, the young physician-naturalist Johann Georg Gmelin and the historian Gerhard Friedrich Müller. The astronomer Louis de l'Isle de la Croyère came from France. The professors selected several of their best Russian students to accompany them as assistants.

Gmelin was to collect plants and animals throughout Siberia and Kamchatka.

Müller's wide-ranging scholarship and orderly scientific view of history made him the most qualified person in St. Petersburg to write his own instructions, virtually defining a new science— ethnography, the description of individual human cultures—in the process. He was to observe the native peoples of Siberia, including Kamchatka, and America, recording their distribution, languages, medicines, weapons, religions, clothes, foods, and customs. He chose to investigate the archives of all Siberian towns, and from these records prepare a history of Siberia. And, finally, he was to write an account of the expedition itself.

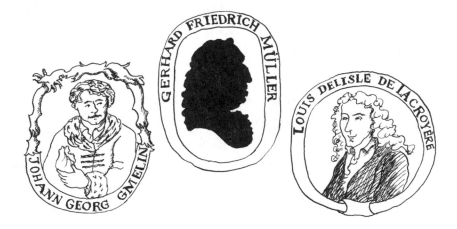

De la Croyère, traveling with ten wagonloads of astronomical equipment, clocks, telescopes, and surveyor's instruments, was to determine the longitude and latitude of all the towns of Siberia and to study the geography of the region. He was the only member of the Academy to have orders to sail to America. Unfortunately, rough roads soon destroyed the precision of his fragile instruments; the clocks lost time and de la Croyère took to drink. Gmelin and Müller preferred to work together, leaving the Frenchman to his own devices.

The Senate ordered Bering to set up a monthly postal service throughout the trackless Siberian wilderness. He was to lay claim to any new lands he might discover, and to establish a trade route across eastern Siberia to the Sea of Okhotsk that did not conflict with the one along the Amur River valley already defined by Russia's treaty with China. The Admiralty expected Bering to construct several lighthouses on rocky promontories jutting out into the seas around Kamchatka, to protect Russian ships.

Captain Martin Spangberg set the expedition in motion with a small advance group, leaving St. Petersburg in February 1733. He was followed in March by the main Admiralty contingent led by Captain Chirikov. Bering left the capital with his family on April 29. In January 1734, the Academy contingent, led by the professors, joined Bering in Tobolsk, the capital of Siberia, after exploring the region near Kazan. Both contingents had the authority to requisition workers, housing, food, building materials, pack animals, guides, and translators in any Siberian town on their route to Okhotsk. However, the farther they went from St. Petersburg, the less likely their requirements were to be met.

Some of the governors of the towns along the way were helpful and interested in the expedition; others were openly hostile; but most simply lacked the resources to satisfy all the expedition's demands. In some parts of Siberia, everything except water and timber was scarce, and sometimes there were over one thousand people traveling with the expedition, all needing to be fed and housed every day. The embryologist Karl Ernst von Baer wrote in 1872 of Bering's accomplishments, "The whole undertaking was planned on so monstrous a scale that under any other chief it would have gone to pieces without any results."

The Admiralty and Academy contingents traveled separately, usually communicating with each other by sending dispatches through the newly established monthly post or by means of couriers who went back and forth to St. Petersburg. The distances were so great that often the two groups were unaware of each other's progress until they happened to meet. Then there were clashes of will and displays of rank as the leaders of both parties quarreled over local resources, though in a dignified way. The officers and the professors each insisted that their status be respected.

When the Academy professors arrived in a town, they felt they were entitled to the most desirable housing. They demanded rooms with chimneys for their artists so that the surface of soot-encrusted

walls did not flake off onto the artists' palettes, turning the colors muddy and dull. The smoky atmosphere of ill-ventilated houses, especially when aggravated by fumes from coal, made the men sick and irritated their eyes.

The naval officers were allowed to have their wives and children with them until they sailed. Bering had left his two older children behind with friends, but the two younger ones, his wife, Anna, and her clavichord accompanied him across Siberia. Spangberg's wife and son traveled with Chirikov until the family could reunite later on the way between Yakutsk and Okhotsk.

Schedules were impossible to maintain in such a wilderness, and the first contingent to arrive in a town monopolized the best available housing. When the second group appeared, they took what was left and then tried to negotiate for better quarters.

Both the Academy and Admiralty contingents enlisted the towns' most highly skilled men—carpenters, blacksmiths, and handlers of horses. Siberian blacksmiths forged shipbuilding tools, metal fittings for the ships and carts, rings of iron to enclose the staves of water barrels, and balls for the ships' cannons. The cannons and anchors required a finer grade of iron and more skilled and experienced craftsmen for their forging. They had been brought across Siberia from Yekaterinburg, an ironworking center. Carpenters built carts and sledges, barges, boats, and ships. Between the

river and the overland routes from Yakutsk to the tiny settlement of Okhotsk stood the way station of Yudoma Krestovskaya, where the carpenters constructed warehouses and storage huts for temporarily holding the tons of anchors, cannons, ropes, sails, food, and clothing necessary for the voyages.

The professors were transporting their library, plant and animal specimens, and the copied paper archives of all the towns in Siberia. Every available means of transport was put to use: barges and flat-bottomed boats for river and lake travel, sledges pulled by dogs or reindeer guided by native Siberian tribesmen, sledges dragged by harnessed men, and laden packhorses for overland travel. Two-thirds of the workers on the expedition were used for transport.

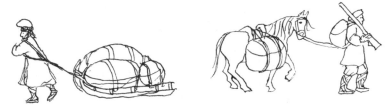

When these workers tried to return to their families, the professors had gallows set up in towns along the way to persuade them to stay with the expedition. Although the professors never actually hung anyone, the state of fear reinforced by the presence of military guards discouraged defection. Still, many workers died from accidents, by sinking in quagmires or being swept away and drowned in rivers; others, stranded by snowstorms on remote trails, died from hunger or exposure to the cold, leaving widows and children without support. Peasants who were taken for the expedition left their fields uncultivated, their farms untended. Failures in the grain harvest followed, and by the end of the expedition the peasants living along the Lena River, in Siberia's richest grain-producing area, were reduced to eating grass and tree bark. It took decades for the towns of Siberia to recover from the effects of the Second Kamchatka Expedition.

3
On to Russia:
Stöller Becomes Steller
ST. PETERSBURG
1734

FULL OF SCIENTIFIC CURIOSITY AND A DESIRE FOR ADVENTURE, Georg Stöller set out for Russia in hopes of joining the expedition. He had only enough money to reach Danzig, on the Baltic Sea. There he signed on as doctor to a Russian Army transport ship, tending wounded soldiers on their way back to St. Petersburg from war in Poland. A stormy winter crossing and near shipwreck in the Gulf of Finland, and the trials of nursing terrified men within the cramped confines of a ship, were his introduction to the seafaring life. It was November 1734 when Stöller delivered the soldiers to the military hospital in St. Petersburg. There his medical responsibility ended. He was eager to see the city and discover what his future held.

Most cities begin as small settlements, grow into villages, then towns, and finally, after many years, attain the size and status of a city. But this natural development did not suit the ardent and impetuous Peter the Great when he determined to move his capital from Moscow to a seaport as close as possible to the rest of Europe.

At tremendous cost, both human and financial, he built a city on marshy land captured from Sweden, where the Neva River flows into the Gulf of Finland. He named it after his patron saint. Perhaps inspired by his beloved Amsterdam, where, as a young man, he had apprenticed himself to a shipbuilder, Peter the Great constructed his new city on islands separated by branches of the Neva. The main avenues were waterways.

GEORG WILHELM STÖLLER

When Stöller arrived in late November 1734, St. Petersburg was only thirty-one years old, yet it was already a fully formed eighteenth-century city, complete with palaces, theaters, a library, and a population of 100,000 people drawn from all over Europe and Asia. In winter, the people skated on the ice or were carried along the frozen waterways in horse-drawn sleds. In summer, boats of all descriptions, from rowboats to royal yachts, were the chief form of transportation. At this time there was only one bridge in St. Petersburg. It was made of boats, lashed together, with planks laid across for ease of dismantling every November, before the Neva froze.

A resident Italian opera company performed in Empress Anna's impressive gold-encrusted theater, which seated a thousand people. The Empress granted free admission to concerts, which occurred four times each week, to any prominent citizen or properly dressed visitor to the city. The entire court of the Empress was present. Having been a choirboy in Windsheim and coming from a musical family, Stöller probably attended these performances.

As a botanist and doctor, however, Stöller probably first set out for the Apothecary Garden near the naval hospital, where medicinal plants were cultivated. There he happened to meet Archbishop Feofan Prokopovich, out for his daily walk. They conversed in Latin,

and Stöller confided his hopes and plans to this wise and sympathetic man. The Archbishop invited him to stay in his palace and become one of his physicians. Georg wrote proudly to his brother Augustin about his prestigious new position, adding that he had changed his name to Steller so that Russians could more easily pronounce it and spell it with their Cyrillic alphabet.

The Archbishop appreciated scholarship and had many friends in the Academy of Sciences. He had studied in Rome, and despite his religious convictions as supreme authority in the Russian Orthodox Church, he enjoyed the company of intelligent learned men of all faiths—or even of none at all. The Archbishop had encouraged Peter the Great to welcome educated Europeans to Russia, and Peter's widow, Catherine I, and his niece Empress Anna continued to solicit his advice.

At the Archbishop's dinner table Steller met members of the Academy of Sciences. They were grateful when this enthusiastic and knowledgeable young man was willing to be involved in their projects. Steller helped the Swiss botanist Dr. Johann Amman to design and plant the Academy's new botanical garden and to catalog its herbarium. Whenever one of the exotic animals in the Imperial Menagerie died, he performed an autopsy—to his own benefit as well as the Academy's: Steller increased his knowledge of anatomy, and the curators of the Imperial Menagerie discovered the cause of death.

Steller spent hours consulting the Academy's superb library. Peter the Great had brought back many extraordinary books as plunder from his wars with Sweden and Poland. This initial collection was continually enlarged by acquisitions of the latest scientific works. On one memorable visit, Steller discovered Mark Catesby's *Natural History of Carolina, Florida and the Bahama Islands*, the first color-plate book of American plants and animals. He was particularly impressed by its illustration of a scolding blue jay from Georgia, a bird unlike any European species.

During the long spring and summer days, Steller roamed the countryside around St. Petersburg with Professor Amman, collecting plants for a flora of the area. One day he returned late to the palace to find a poem on his desk. It was by the Archbishop, who pretended that he had died and been buried while Steller was off botanizing, to the neglect of his duties as physician. It begins:

While the good Steller goes searching for medical plants for the sick,
The pitiful patient departs this life by a lingering death . . .

The poem ends with Steller raging against Fate for having dared to take his patient during his absence. The Archbishop seems to have known how to tease Steller by gently recognizing his foibles without hurting his feelings.

As preparation for the post he hoped to be given on the Second Kamchatka Expedition, Steller tried to find books about Siberia,

but next to nothing had been published. Fortunately, he discovered Daniel Gottlieb Messerschmidt living in reclusive poverty with his young wife and seven-year-old daughter. Dr. Messerschmidt had traveled for eight years in Siberia, west of the Lena River, under orders from Peter the Great. He returned to St. Petersburg in 1727 with wagonloads of Siberian artifacts, natural history specimens, mineral samples, and notebooks full of observations.

Messerschmidt was an all-round naturalist, anthropologist, archaeologist, geologist, and historian. During the Second Kamchatka Expedition, the range of studies undertaken by Messerschmidt alone was divided between Gmelin and Müller. Today they would require many specialists.

Messerschmidt returned to St. Petersburg in a shattered state of health. Terrible bouts of fever, long Siberian winters, and the infuriating frustration of dealing with uncooperative Russian officials in remote outposts had taken their toll. A year after his return, he was forced by the Senate to give his collections to the recently founded Academy of Sciences. Then he married Brigitta Helena von Boeckler, described as "a lively, wild woman who was quite his opposite." He spent his few remaining years writing up his notes and sorting his vast collections. Steller learned as much as he could about Siberia from him, but their brief friendship lasted no more than three months, for in 1735 Messerschmidt died.

Soon after they left St. Petersburg in August of 1733, Professors Gmelin and Müller had realized the immensity of their undertaking. They also saw that de la Croyère was hopeless as a geographer but for political reasons would have to continue on the expedition. They requested that the Academy send two more scholars to carry out part of their work in Siberia: one for chemistry, mining, and natural history, and the other for astronomy and geography. The Academy agreed to their request. Professor Amman and the Archbishop used their considerable influence to help Steller gain one of the positions. The second post was not filled until 1741.

On July 28, 1736, the Academy proposed to the Senate that Georg Steller be appointed an adjunct professor to the Second Kamchatka Expedition. As an adjunct Steller would have a lower rank than a professor, and he would be serving under a man his own age—Johann Gmelin, whom he had never met. But Steller was grateful for the appointment. He may have hoped that one of the professors would be ready to return to St. Petersburg, allowing Steller to take over his responsibilities. In any case, Steller would be unsupervised until he joined the professors in the town of Yeniseisk, on the Yenisei River in central Siberia. Six weeks after Steller had been proposed, his most understanding friend and supporter in St. Petersburg, Archbishop Feofan, died quietly on September 19, 1736. On February 7, 1737, the Academy confirmed Steller's appointment and swore him to secrecy concerning any discoveries he might make while in its pay. The locations of mineral deposits of gold, silver, copper, iron, or tin, of safe trade routes, and of native sources for fur were valuable knowledge that Russia did not wish to share with other nations.

Steller spent the next year preparing for his journey. He examined the specimens and manuscripts that Professor Gmelin had already sent from Siberia. He assembled scientific instruments and medical supplies unobtainable beyond the Ural Mountains, and reams of paper for painting natural history subjects and for mounting pressed plants and dried fish skins. He finished his work on the Academy's flora of the St. Petersburg area while courting Dr. Messerschmidt's young widow, Brigitta Helena.

Having heard her late husband's frightening tales of Siberian travel, Brigitta Helena very reluctantly agreed to marry Steller and set off with him on the expedition. In November 1737, they were married. Steller never told his family back in Germany; they learned of his marriage only after his death.

After Christmas, Steller and his new wife, accompanied by Brigitta Helena's daughter, spent two weeks traveling by troika to Moscow, wrapped in furs. Other troikas traveled with them, carrying the many supplies for the expedition and Steller's artist, Johann Cornelius Decker. By the time they arrived, Steller's wife had

changed her mind and decided to spend a year in Moscow before returning with her daughter to St. Petersburg. Steller gave her money and furniture and agreed to support her with half of his salary while he was on the expedition. In May 1738, Steller set out in melancholy spirits on the great adventure of his life.

ST. PETERSBURG

4
Steller's
Journey Begins
SIBERIA
1738–1739

IN THE SUMMER OF 1738, STELLER CROSSED THE URAL
Mountains into an astonishing Asian landscape. The mountains
acted as an ecological barrier: to the west were the European flora
and fauna Steller knew so well; to the east were plants and animals
he had seen only as dried or stuffed specimens in the collections of
Gmelin and Messerschmidt—to say nothing of many more as yet
unknown to science. It was all wonderfully unfamiliar; there was so
much to collect. Steller vowed to return another year in the spring,
when different plants would be in bloom.

In Tobolsk he met his escort, Aleksei Fedorovich Danilov,
who stayed with him for most of the next eight years, acting as
hunter, guide, and translator for Steller, who was still learning
Russian.

Although new roads were being built, rivers remained the best
way to travel through much of Siberia. The areas between them
were often densely forested, mountainous, or boggy, making progress slow, especially with heavy baggage.

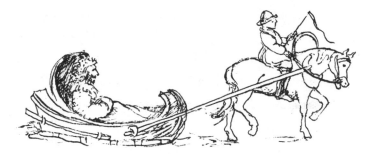

Horse-drawn sledges on the frozen rivers were the easiest and safest form of transportation, although the winter weather was extremely cold and snowy. At intervals along the way there were government huts, uncomfortable windowless shelters with frozen dirt floors, with stables where tired horses could be exchanged for fresh ones. In spring and summer, after the river ice had broken up and flowed downstream, it was often dangerous to entrust a boat to the swift current. Travel upstream, with harnessed porters hauling the boat with towlines from the riverbank or the shallows of the riverbed, was slow enough to match the pace of a naturalist walking alongside. It offered perfect opportunities for collecting specimens.

Steller spent his first summer on the expedition walking beside the Irtysh and Ob rivers on his way to meet Gmelin and Müller in Yeniseisk. In the long light-filled evenings of the far north he wrote up his observations, made dissections, and mounted his pressed plants and large dried fish skins on paper. (Smaller fish might be preserved in alcohol, but glass jars were fragile, easily broken in transport, and often unavailable.) Steller's artist, Johann Cornelius Decker, had traveled with him from St. Petersburg; he painted nearby, recording the living colors of the flowers or fish before they were permanently altered by desiccation.

Excited by everything he saw, Steller was eager to travel all the way to Kamchatka. The professors, however, after five years of hardship, were in a very different frame of mind and were ready to go home.

Across Siberia, Professor Gmelin had collected thousands of plants and animals that his artists, Johann Christian Berckhan and Johann Wilhelm Lürsenius, had painted in watercolor. Every so often he would send packing cases full of specimens and manuscripts back to the Academy in St. Petersburg, where they were carefully opened and preserved. In 1736, while staying in Yakutsk, Gmelin returned from a party to find that his house had burned to the ground; all of his manuscripts and collections from the previous year were destroyed. He was relieved to find that his supply of Rhenish wine had survived the flames.

Professor Müller had spent his time compiling a history of Siberia by delving into the archives of the region's cities and towns.

On the basis of these documents and interviews with native shamans, he was able to compare the Russians' differing treatment of various Siberian peoples. Müller collected tribal artifacts and recorded native languages. He hired local men to dig up ancient burial mounds, some dating back to the Scythians, so that he could glean historical and cultural information. But now Müller was suffering from poor health.

In keeping with his instructions from the Senate, Bering had been very helpful to Professors Gmelin and Müller at the beginning of the expedition. He built and outfitted a commodious barque in Tver on the Volga River for their comfortable voyage to Kazan in 1733. But four years later Bering was struggling with the soaring costs of the expedition. Before leaving St. Petersburg in 1733, he had estimated a budget of 10,000 to 12,000 rubles for the cost of the expedition, not including salaries, shipbuilding, or provisions. By 1737, the actual costs had run over 40,000 rubles each year, and he had nothing to show for it. The professors were critical of Bering and the progress of the expedition under his leadership, even sending their complaints back to the Senate in St. Petersburg. When the professors wrote to Bering to make sure he could provide suitable food and cabins on board ship for their voyage from Okhotsk to Kamchatka, Bering replied that he was barely able to take care of his own men; the professors must look after themselves. For the professors, this was the last straw.

They wrote to the Senate from Yakutsk. Müller requested permission to attempt to restore his health in a milder climate; Gmelin asked to be allowed to replace his destroyed collections by retracing his steps through Siberia to St. Petersburg. At the same time he wrote to a friend at the Academy, offering to send a gift of money for the secretary of the Senate if it might hasten his recall to St. Petersburg. (The bribe might not have been necessary, but his request *was* granted in July 1742.) If Bering could not assure them of comfort, ample food, and the deference appropriate to their positions, the professors preferred to return home. While waiting to hear from the Academy, they assigned their work in Kamchatka to their most promising and enterprising Russian student, Stepan Petrovich Krasheninnikov, and sent him over the mountains to Okhotsk. Hoping for word from St. Petersburg, the professors made their way along the Lena River, then by sledge to Irkutsk, where they overwintered. In the spring, they voyaged along the Angara and Yenisei rivers. Disembarking in Yeniseisk on August 25, 1738, they learned that Steller had not yet arrived.

On October 4, 1737, Krasheninnikov had set sail from the port of Okhotsk for the volcanic peninsula of Kamchatka, under orders from Professors Gmelin and Müller. The ship was the rotting *Fortuna*, constructed for Bering's First Kamchatka Expedition ten years earlier. She had barely left the shelter of the harbor when she began to sink. Krasheninnikov wrote an account of the *Fortuna*'s last voyage:

We saw that our ship was taking on a great deal of water, so that the men down in the hold were standing in water up to their knees. Although two pumps were used constantly and everyone bailed water with pots and kettles and anything he could find, the amount of water did not diminish. The ship was so heavily laden that the water was already coming in through the port-holes. The only way to save ourselves was to lighten the ship.

They first jettisoned everything on deck—clothes, food, and scientific instruments—and then threw overboard about four hundred *puds* (more than seven tons) of cargo, "taken at random," to raise the ship in the water. Pumping and bailing night and day, they succeeded in reaching the mouth of the Bolshaya River in Kamchatka, near the settlement of Bolsheretsk, after ten days of cold, rain, and snow. Krasheninnikov described their battle with the "outgoing tide" and "foaming waves":

The men were in despair. These waves were so wild that they swept right over the ship, which was very badly split in many places . . . We were cast up on shore . . .

As he stepped ashore, Krasheninnikov was thrown to the ground by an earthquake, the first of many he was to experience during his three years in Kamchatka.

The next day we found nothing but the planks from the wreckage of our ship; the rest had been swept away by the sea. Then we saw the full extent of the danger which had faced us, for all the ship's planks were black, and so rotten that one could easily break them by hand.

In Bolsheretsk, Krasheninnikov carefully followed Gmelin and Müller's detailed instructions with the help of his two servants, who had come with him on the *Fortuna*, and a few hunters. His main task was preparing for the possible arrival of the professors by

building several houses, laying out a kitchen vegetable garden, and stabling reindeer as a winter food supply. Then he traveled by raft, snowshoe, and dogsled throughout the peninsula, mapping its volcanoes, rivers, and coastline. He studied the Kamchadals—or Itelmen, as they were also called—eating their foods and recording their medicines, customs, hunting techniques, and religious beliefs. On his return to Bolsheretsk, he set out the living

plants he had collected in the garden. Krasheninnikov wrote up his observations as he awaited the arrival of the spring packet boat from Okhotsk, which might bring the professors—or at least their further instructions. But the professors did not come. It would be three years before Krasheninnikov saw anyone from the Academy, and then it would be Georg Steller.

By November of 1738, Steller
had reached the important trading
city of Tomsk, in western Siberia,
which, like many Siberian towns,
had no resident doctor. Whenever
Steller arrived in a settlement, the
entire ailing population, upon learning that he was a physician as well

as a naturalist, would descend upon him, begging for treatment.
Contaminated water caused by poor sanitation was rife with deadly
organisms. After treating many patients, Steller caught a severe
fever just as the Tomsk winter set in. Decker and Danilov were
afraid he might die, and wrote to the professors in Yeniseisk ask-

ing permission to postpone their
departure; a feverish man might not
survive a ten-day journey in tem-
peratures going down to more than
40 degrees below zero Fahrenheit,
sledging by day and spending his
nights in miserable government
huts. Gmelin and Müller readily
agreed; they needed Steller to finish

Krasheninnikov's work in Kamchatka for them. By January 1739,
Steller was well enough to join them in Yeniseisk.

The professors might have been startled by Steller's backwoods
appearance, but they were very glad to see him. He spent seven
weeks in their company, sharing his discoveries and admiring
theirs. He consulted their extensive natural history library. (Steller
had traveled too rough to bring with him more than a few hand-
books.) The professors enjoyed rather greater amenities. It was not
merely in dress and equipage that one could tell the academician
from the adjunct.

Gmelin and Steller had been born within months of each other in small cities less than one hundred miles apart. Both came from well-educated Lutheran families of similar social status, but the two naturalists could not have been more different in temperament and style.

A brilliant, easygoing, and lovable botanist and doctor, Gmelin dressed in the elegant attire of an academician, complete with wig, embroidered waistcoat, and highly polished boots. He was fond of good food and fine wine and, while willing to do his duty, much preferred comfort to hardship. In short, he expected to have the luxuries of St. Petersburg in the wilds of Siberia.

Steller had no such metropolitan tastes; the contrast between the two men was striking. Gmelin described Steller this way:

He was not troubled about his clothing. As it is necessary in Siberia to carry along one's own housekeeping outfit, he had reduced it to the least possible compass. His drinking cup for beer was the same as his cup for mead and whiskey. Wine he dispensed with entirely. He had only one dish out of which he ate and in which was served all his food. For this he needed no chef. He cooked everything himself, and that with so little circumstance that soup, vegetables and meat were put into the same pot and boiled together. Smoke and smell in the room in which he worked did not affect him. He used no wig and no powder; any kind of shoe or boot suited him . . . It was no hardship for him to go hungry and thirsty a whole day if he was able to accomplish something advantageous to science.

Gmelin and Müller, the itinerant professors, carried with them a sort of traveling university, complete with artists, students, and library. They brought kegs of Rhenish wine and chefs to cook their food. Steller had only his artist, his guide, and the animals he had tamed along the way, including a roe deer and two cormorants. All three men traveled with horses and porters, but Steller needed far fewer than the professors.

The presence or absence of an anthropologist and historian such as Müller was of little concern to Steller, but the company of a naturalist was quite a different matter. If Gmelin would only return to St. Petersburg, Steller could continue to work as he had on his way to Yeniseisk—alone and without supervision. After all, he had received his orders from the Academy in St. Petersburg—what more did he need?

The professors were impressed by Steller's collections and over-joyed by his willingness to go to Kamchatka in their place. After two years, they had only just received a first letter from Krasheninnikov describing the destruction of the *Fortuna* and the insects, volcanoes, earthquakes, and manifold discomforts of Kamchatka. When Steller was informed of the dangers he would be facing, the professors found him even more intent on setting out. He relished a challenge, perhaps sensing that it brought out his best qualities. When Gmelin's biographer compared the two men, he observed that this *Sonntagskind*, Steller, was "passionately in love with science; tough and indefatigable."

The professors, assuming they would soon be recalled to St. Petersburg, exchanged their highly accomplished artist Johann Christian Berckhan for Steller's less adept Johann Cornelius Decker, and assigned one of their students, Aleksei Gorlanov, to write Steller's official correspondence in Russian. Steller wrote all of his scientific observations and descriptions in Latin and never became adept at writing Russian. To help Steller catalog the new plants and animals he had found, they gave him some books from their natural history library. Then they instructed him to join Krasheninnikov in Kamchatka as soon as possible.

Steller left the professors in March 1739. By May, he was writing to Gmelin expressing excitement over his investigations and discoveries:

I have compared the muscles of the crow with those of the crane in order to find out whether they may not be the same in all birds as to number and position and only different in form. Among the fishes I have also undertaken similar comparative studies especially with regard to the rays and the position of their muscles.

The lonely melancholy he had experienced when his wife left him now gave way to other feelings. He described a small crustacean from the Angara River and a louse on a crow and then made a confession regarding his wife: "I have entirely forgotten her and fallen in love with Nature."

The Barguzin Mountains
1739–1740

5

STELLER MADE GOOD TIME ON THE NEW ROAD FROM YENI-seisk to Irkutsk, traveling eight hundred miles in two weeks. He arrived in the spring of 1739, hoping to assemble provisions and leave for Yakutsk in June. But Bering's naval contingent had recently passed through the town, taking all the workers, food, building materials, and pack animals the people could spare. So instead of going on to Yakutsk, Steller decided to climb the unexplored Barguzin Mountains during the summer and spend the winter putting his collections in order, leaving for Okhotsk and Kamchatka the following spring. He wrote to Gmelin, explaining his change of plans.

In a large, flat, raft-like boat called a *doshchenik*, Steller crossed the vast and mysterious Lake Baikal—to the native people it was known as "the Holy Sea." He observed the large colony of seals living in this

extremely deep freshwater lake, more than a thousand miles south of their near relatives in the Arctic Ocean.

Steller tested the medicinal and nutritional properties of the plants near the lake. He found a new species of wheatgrass from which oozed a thick brown liquid that tasted like honey. Collecting a tablespoon of it to stir into his tea, he drank it with pleasure.

He went on from Lake Baikal to ascend the Barguzin Mountains, which rose from the steppe like a wall six thousand feet high. At the highest altitudes he discovered a beautiful flower to which he assigned an almost mystical significance. He refers to it affectionately as "our gentian."

The view fairly overwhelmed me . . . Dwarf cedars, dwarf birches, elders and lowly willows creeping humbly along the ground gird the highest tops like garlands on the bald head of an

old man. The summit or crest of the mountain . . . did not boast
a single shrub or tree; it was covered only with an endless expanse
of gray mosses like a blanket nearly a foot thick. In the very center rocks of immense size surrounded a lake of the purest water,
but destitute of fishes or other living creatures . . . Among these

rocks and along the moss-covered
shore of the lake our gentian was
found . . . of a most peculiar
coloration . . . resembling the
diaphanous air-bladder of fishes
variegated with bluish and greenish
stripes and spots.

I myself, stimulated by the rarefaction of the air and the
strangeness of the place, felt as if in a wonderful dream and under
such a spell as I remember to have experienced when for the first
time, at Stolberg, deep underground, I gazed down into the abyss
of the Stolbergian mines.

Another plant discovered by Steller was the lovely but toxic
pale primrose yellow *Rhododendron chrysanthum*. In his biography of
the naturalist, Leonhard Stejneger described what Steller witnessed:

When a tame roebuck that
lived with him ate around ten of its
leaves, astonishingly, after several
minutes, the animal began to caper,
to stagger, and to jerk its head. In
about seven minutes it fell forward
on its knees, trying vainly to rise,
nor did a dose of milk mend matters, but for four hours it lay overcome by a deep stupor like a

drunkard, apparently terrified by dreams and repeatedly seized by trembling. When at last the stupor wore off, it was as lively as before, but never again did it accept the offer of a rhododendron [leaf].

Steller wrote to Gmelin describing what he had accomplished in his many fields of investigation. He had already collected sixty different species of birds, one hundred insects, and more than a thousand plants, carefully noting the date, location, and habitat of each one. He was developing a theory concerning the effect of the environment on the distribution of plants and needed accurate information to prove or disprove it. He asked native shamans about their medicinal and hallucinogenic plants and fungi and recorded their information.

He also studied the minerals around Lake Baikal, collecting rock samples and analyzing their content. He would be neglecting his duty to the Senate if he failed to recognize valuable mineral deposits. He was also interested in the native human populations.

The twelfth item on his list of occupations and discoveries was this:

Beginning of a Russian, Greek and Latin Dictionary of Natural History, with which I try to keep Gorlanov busy when he has nothing else to do.

Knowing that the student Gorlanov had helped Müller with such tasks, Steller assigned him to gather vocabulary from the native Tungus people.

Every aspect of the natural world fascinated Steller. While collecting various birds, he devised a new technique for preserving the minute parasites living on their feathers. He placed the insects between thin sheets of clear mica and studied them through his microscope, observing their tiny structures. Seventy-four years later, a German biologist, viewing Steller's mica slides in St. Petersburg, wrote that the insects looked so fresh "they can be drawn and described as if they were alive."

Steller returned to Irkutsk in September 1739 to prepare for the journey to Yakutsk and Kamchatka. He hired local people to build rafts and sew leather bags to keep food and clothing dry for the trip down the Lena River. He arranged for sixty horses to be well tended through the winter months so that they could carry heavy loads for him in the spring. In a letter to Gmelin, he wrote that he had so much to do during the day that he did not have time to eat.

By now Steller needed to replenish his supply of paper for painting and pressing plants and fish skins. Accompanied by only a few servants, and changing drivers in villages along the way, he crossed Lake Baikal once again—this time on its frozen surface, in sledges—and went south to buy Chinese paper in the market town of Kyakhta on the Russian-Chinese border. He arrived there in time for the Chinese New Year celebrations. Although it was midwinter, he collected seeds along the way from dried stalks wherever plants peeked above the snow.

He traveled on to Yakutsk, where he had his fortune told during a traditional shamanistic ceremony. After going into a trance, the shaman told Steller things about his past. Then he predicted that Steller would sail beyond Kamchatka to discover an unknown people not yet under the yoke of the Russian Empire.

6
Provisioning
the
Expedition
MARCH 1733–JUNE 1734

WHILE STELLER WAS TRAVELING ACROSS SIBERIA, AND Müller and Gmelin's student Stepan Krasheninnikov was occupied in Kamchatka, a member of the Admiralty contingent, Captain Martin Spangberg, was charting and exploring more southerly lands—the Kuril Islands and Japan. Both he and Captain Chirikov played important roles during the Siberian years of the expedition.

Martin Pedersen Spangberg, Bering's second-in-command throughout both the First and Second Kamchatka Expeditions, was a brilliant navigator and a man of forceful character. During his lifetime his name was blackened by the regional commander of Okhotsk, who was trying to conceal his own misdeeds, and, uncharacteristically, by Aleksei Chirikov, who usurped Spangberg's claim to leadership of the expedition after the death of their commanding officer.

With the possible exception of Bering himself, Georg Steller and Martin Spangberg suffered more than any other members of the expedition from slander and false accusations. They came under attack for similar reasons. Both were foreign-born and therefore aroused the suspicion and jealousy of some Russian officials, and both defended native peoples against the abuse of these same men in authority. Unlike Steller, whose name was cleared shortly before his death, Captain Spangberg had to wait until the end of the twentieth century before a just assessment of his character and accomplishments was finally presented.

Spangberg and Bering were fellow Danes, and during the First Kamchatka Expedition they were of the same mind on August 13, 1728, when Bering held a ship's council at sea to determine their winter course. Captain Bering, Captain Lieutenant Spangberg, and Lieutenant Chirikov were the three officers on board the *St. Gabriel.* They had to decide whether to sail farther north or to return to port. Continuing the voyage would entail overwintering either in an ice-locked sea or on land with the notoriously warlike Chukchi tribe. As they sailed into the Chukchi Sea from what we now call the Bering Sea, Spangberg and Bering thought the risks of encountering icebergs or running aground in the dark and fog were becoming too great. They had (they believed) already fulfilled Peter the Great's order to sail far enough north to determine that Asia and America were separate landmasses. Lieutenant Aleksei Chirikov, the highest-ranking Russian on the expedition but third-in-command (having joined the Russian Navy a year after Spangberg), disagreed with his superior officers. Reaching a European settlement was also part of Peter the Great's instructions. Chirikov therefore proposed that they should sail west along the coast of northern Siberia until they reached the Russian settlement at the mouth of the Kolyma River. In the Russian Navy, sailing decisions were made by majority vote of the officers. Bering and Spangberg's choice prevailed, but the wisdom of that choice has been disputed, often with patriotic fervor, from the time the expedition returned to St. Petersburg in 1730 until the present day.

During the three years between the expeditions, first Spangberg and then Chirikov was promoted to captain. Captain Martin Spangberg, the first member of the Second Kamchatka Expedition to depart for Siberia, left St. Petersburg in February 1733. On the basis of information gathered during the First Expedition, the Senate and the Admiralty made demands upon the governors of the Siberian towns through which the Second Expedition would pass. Spangberg's first assignment was to make sure that these demands were being fulfilled. He traveled swiftly, accompanied by only ten men.

One of the lessons learned from the First Kamchatka Expedition was that men needed more food than had been allotted if they were to survive the rigors of dragging sledges and hauling barges in the freezing climate of Siberia. The food allowance was therefore doubled for workers on the Second Kamchatka Expedition. When they were at sea they received double wages as well.

The main Admiralty contingent of around five hundred men, women, and children, under the command of Captain Chirikov, left St. Petersburg without Bering on March 18, 1733. Bering departed five weeks later and joined his men and Spangberg on May 14 in Tver. They spent a month preparing riverboats for sailing down the Volga, and by July 25 they had all reached Kazan. Spangberg went

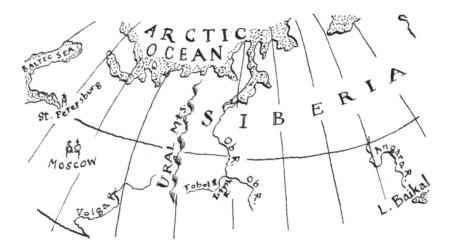

ahead with his small group, purchasing food and shipbuilding materials. Two of the heaviest items had to travel the longest distance. The massive sails and sailcloth came from the Admiralty in St. Petersburg, as did most of the rope for the ships. The anchors and cannons were transported from the forge at the recently built Siberian mining town of Yekaterinburg.

Most of the rye flour for the expedition came from the region surrounding Ilimsk, between the upper Angara and Lena rivers. Spangberg selected army officers to oversee the forced gathering of tons of grain for bread and ship's biscuit. He then traveled down the Lena to the province of Yakutsk, home of the Sakha tribe. The Sakha herdsmen—known to this day for the hardiness of their animals and the skill with which they breed and tend them—provided cattle and packhorses. Some of the beef would be eaten at once; much would be preserved with salt for the voyages; and some of the cattle would be herded by Sakha cattlemen over the mountains to Okhotsk.

Suspecting that men and horses might never return from the expedition, some governors contributed weak or decrepit workers and animals. Often the amount of food and building materials fell short of the huge demands made by the Senate. Spangberg would

try to make up for it in the next settlement or send word of the
shortfall to Bering or Chirikov, who might find the resources in
other towns.

The amassing of weapons, the seasoning of lumber, and the
making of masts were but a few of the preparations necessary for
the construction of sledges, barges, and ships for Bering's explorations. Spangberg was instructed to buy thousands of saddlebags
for the packhorses. When he found carpenters or blacksmiths, he
hired them and sent them to where Bering or Chirikov would next
need them.

And so he went on, hiring men and floating, dragging, or
sledging cargo thousands of miles across Siberia. Captain Chirikov
followed in his wake, building boats, gathering provisions, and fin-
ishing the work Spangberg had begun. On the upper Lena,
Chirikov's workers—now numbering 700—constructed 121 riverboats for shipping 750 tons of provisions and 70 tons of other supplies to Yakutsk. Meanwhile, Bering was en route to Irkutsk with a
small contingent, including his family.

Although Spangberg traveled rapidly, he did not reach Yakutsk
until May of 1734. He left for Okhotsk three weeks later. Bering
did not arrive in Yakutsk until four months after Spangberg's departure for Okhotsk, and Chirikov did not arrive until a year later.

7
Captain Martin Spangberg: Okhotsk, the Kuril Islands, and Japan
1734–1741

O N THE HARROWING ROUTE TO OKHOTSK, CAPTAIN SPANG-berg's troubles with Major General Grigorij Grigorievitch Skornyakov-Pisarev, the commander of the region, began. As a favorite of Peter the Great, Pisarev had held the posts of police director and head of the Naval Academy in St. Petersburg until he conspired to murder the powerful minister Prince Menshikov in 1727. The plot was discovered and he was knouted, branded with a hot iron, and exiled to Siberia. However, the Russian government sometimes chose to make use of its political exiles. In 1731, the Senate appointed Pisarev to govern Okhotsk and to make preparations for the arrival of the Second Kamchatka Expedition. He was ordered to increase the population by settling Tungus tribesmen in the area. Under Pisarev's supervision, these new residents were to start growing grain, building a shipyard and quay, and constructing ships to be used for trans-

porting merchants and furs back and forth across the Sea of
Okhotsk to the Kamchatkan port of Bolsheretsk.

The 750 miles from Yakutsk to Okhotsk were the most grueling of Spangberg's expedition, at least on land. Harnessed men
faced the prospects of exhaustion, starvation, and freezing to death
as they struggled to pull ships in ice-cold river water. Their horses
went lame crossing the stony riverbeds, or sank to their death in
the horrible quagmires near Yudoma Krestovskaya. Along the
route, the Senate had ordered Pisarev to build stables, warming

huts, and storage sheds for food to protect the hundreds of porters
and horses carrying many tons of provisions and ships' materials
over a long period of time. Pisarev had had three years to make
these arrangements but did nothing. Indeed, he had not even both-
ered to come to Okhotsk.

After the long winter journey, during which almost all of his
hundred horses died of starvation, Spangberg found the town of
Okhotsk unchanged from the last time he had seen it—at the end
of the First Kamchatka Expedition. The only difference was that
now the population was suffering from famine. Spangberg evenly
distributed state-owned provisions and the food he had brought for
his men. Then he set to work building the town and shipyard that
Pisarev had neglected to construct. When Pisarev finally arrived, he
and Spangberg were at loggerheads. While the captain was eager to
build his ships and sail off on his voyages, the regional commander,

a jealous and disgruntled exile, had no intention of helping him—a foreigner—attain fame and glory through successful explorations.

Both men wrote dispatches to the Senate. Unfortunately, Spangberg had a hot temper, triggered by righteous indignation. Pisarev once reported that he had dared to hit a Russian carpenter for stealing (and then denying he had stolen) a native Sakha's cow. Spangberg, on the other hand, could point out that Pisarev had fulfilled none of the Senate's orders and continued to obstruct the progress of the expedition. From Yakutsk, Bering recommended patience and diplomacy to Spangberg, two qualities he himself was unable to employ when his turn came to deal with Pisarev. The Senate in St. Petersburg sorted through the pile of allegations and decided in favor of Spangberg. They directed that he should be the commanding officer of Okhotsk until he was ready to sail. Pisarev finally left town when Spangberg threatened to lock him up. Without the old regional commander, both the building of the town and the construction of the ships progressed rapidly. In the new shipyard, Spangberg's men refitted one of the vessels from the First Kamchatka Expedition, the *St. Gabriel*, and constructed two others, the *Archangel Michael* and the *Nadezhda (Hope)* for his own voyages. When these were completed, Spangberg began the simultaneous construction of twin ships for Bering's voyages to Kamchatka and America.

But two circumstances involving provisions delayed Spangberg's departure for the Kuril Islands. In the autumn of 1737, just
before the Okhotsk harbor became icebound, Krasheninnikov had
sailed for Kamchatka, taking most of the town's provisions with
him. While Spangberg was in Okhotsk, Captain Chirikov was detailed to organize the sending of provisions and ships' materials
from the midway storage depot of Yudoma Krestovskaya. Spangberg and Chirikov had not been of one mind during the First Kamchatka Expedition; now they locked horns again. Spangberg was
outraged when Chirikov chose to send by dogsled seven thousand
pounds of rope for Bering and Chirikov's voyage to America, the
ships for which were still unfinished, rather than the food Spangberg needed immediately for his voyage to Japan. As a result,
Spangberg missed a sailing season, delaying his voyage by a year.

Spangberg had to stop work on Bering's ships in order to gather
together enough food for the winter. He sent some of his men back
over the mountains to Yakutsk for new provisions while others
caught and preserved fish, the only readily available food. Soon
Bering arrived with the workers and men for his expedition and
continued construction of the unfinished ships, naming them the
St. Peter and the St. Paul.

When the ice in the harbor broke up in June of the following
year, 1738, Captain Spangberg's three vessels sailed from Okhotsk,
leaving Bering to complete preparations for his own voyages.

On June 16, 1738, Spangberg and his 151 men sailed in three
ships for Kamchatka. Three weeks later, after obtaining more provisions from the storehouses in Bolsheretsk, they began charting the
four hundred miles of the Kuril Island chain. In his report to the
Admiralty, Spangberg described the dangerous conditions: "the sea
mist is thick and the currents are fierce. Strong gales occur often,
the weather is unpredictable, and things happen which are not seen
in other seas."

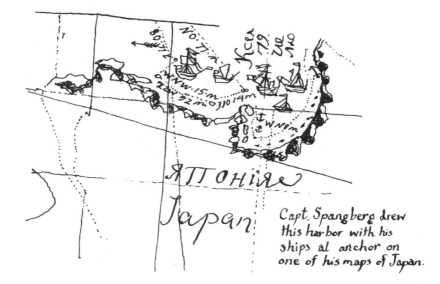

Capt. Spangberg drew
this harbor with his
ships at anchor on
one of his maps of Japan.

It was not only the seas that could be strange and unwelcoming. From the year 1603, the leaders of Japan, the Tokugawa Shogunate, had allowed only limited contact with the Chinese, the Koreans, and the Dutch. Trade and relations with any other people were strictly forbidden. The Japanese had prospered as a virtually closed society. In spite of this policy, Spangberg and his men were treated with polite kindness by the Kuril Islanders. After Spangberg's men decorated their ships with flags to attract attention, Japanese fishermen rowed out to the ships, bringing fish. Other islanders brought rice, salted cucumbers, and daikons, and even climbed on board. But as soon as the Russian ships left their waters, the islanders sent reports of the encounter to Edo (now known as Tokyo). The Russians had been instructed by their Senate, which was acquainted with the isolationist policy of the shogunate, to try to initiate friendly trade relations. But the Japanese were cautious; they did not want to be accused of welcoming forbidden foreigners.

Spangberg described the fishing vessels: "The boats have decks, and on these are built boxes for water, and on the deck were built ovens with pots for cooking porridge, and to enable them to stay on

board overnight when at sea." He noted that the hulls were sheathed with copper. (His own ships were protected by a coating of pitch.)

He observed the islanders' hair and dress:

> These Japanese are middle and small-sized . . . They are bare-footed, none of them wear trousers. The hair on the front part of the head down to the forehead has been cut off and fastened with glue further down, the hair behind is gathered into a little tuft pointing forward. They have large, flat hats made of grass which those wearing a hat bind under the cheek; but those who do not wear a hat bind a scarf round their head.

Probably on the eastern cape of Hokkaido, Spangberg encountered the Ainu for the first time.

Their faces are like those of the Kuril people; their clothes are long and coloured with pieces of oriental silks sewn unto them; they are barefooted and have hairy legs and bodies; they have big beards, long and black, and the elderly men have grey hairs in their beards and hair. Some of them have silver rings in their ears.

We are fortunate to have eyewitnesses from both the Russian and the Japanese sides of the encounter.

Zenbei, probably a minor local official, sent this description of Spangberg's men to Edo:

> Their clothes seemed to be made of wool. They wore black shirts and black shoes and also something resembling the Japanese "haori" (semi long coat). The clothes reached their knees and were loosened at four points. At the breast and stomach they were buttoned. All of the eight men were as tall as 1.8 m [5 feet 11 inches] or more. When they took off their caps, you could see their hair which was blond and cut short. The stubble was visible. Their skin had the same colour as ours. Their eyes were reddish and looked like those of apes. Their appearance looked strange but they seemed to be gentle, so we did not consider taking them prisoners.

Zenbei must have noticed the ship's cannons: "There was an iron pipe . . . it was like a huge Chinese bamboo with joints in both ends and a small hole in the top. There were four of these."

A Buddhist priest, who must have previously encountered Europeans but not a globe, wrote a slightly different account:

> The sailors looked like Dutchmen with reddish (blond?) hair and different caps. Their noses were big and sharp, their eyes were bright. However their bodies were quite ordinary. Their clothes resembled

those worn by Dutchmen. The officers wore red, woollen clothes, while most of the others wore leather clothes. There were four dogs and many cormorants on board . . . A leather ball was seen with maps drawn in black of various countries.

Between 1738 and 1739, Spangberg made two voyages, mapping many of the Kuril Islands and part of Japan. By the time he reached Japan on his second voyage, thirteen of his men, including the ship's doctor, had died of scurvy. Spangberg hastened back to Okhotsk.

Russian tax collectors already received *yasak* (tax payment) in the form of fur seal pelts from the people living on the northernmost Kuril Islands. The Senate's list of objectives for the Second Kamchatka Expedition had included an instruction "to search for new lands and islands not yet conquered and to bring them under subjection." Spangberg had therefore proposed extending Russian control and taxation all the way to Japan, by force if necessary. But now the Senate decreed that friendly trading arrangements were its goal, both in Japan and in America. Gifts were to be given, and no violence was to be employed.

Spangberg's new maps of the Kuril Islands were far more accurate than any previously made. Bering sent Spangberg to St. Petersburg to report directly to the Senate on the success of his voyage. There he would receive a new assignment. But Spangberg had jealous enemies at work, especially Pisarev, who had resented his demands and disliked him personally. Behind his back, Pisarev sent a report to St. Petersburg claiming that the captain had gone no farther than Korea and had not reached Japan at all.

Traveling through Siberia, on July 8, 1740, Spangberg was met on the upper Lena River by a messenger from Empress Anna. Remembering that Pisarev had once been head of the Naval Academy, the Empress acted on his report, ordering Spangberg to confirm his charts by following the arc of the Kuril Islands to Japan again.

Meanwhile, in Yakutsk, Steller had heard rumors of Spangberg's latest voyage. In the excitement of the moment, he wrote to the Senate asking permission to go on the next expedition to Japan as soon as he had completed his duties in Kamchatka.

On the way back to Okhotsk, a disgruntled Spangberg happened to overtake Steller, coming from Yakutsk. The two continued their journey together on horseback, their baggage trains following at a slower pace. Spangberg fascinated the young naturalist with his traveler's tales of encounters with Ainu covered with thick hair, and fish that no European had ever seen. Steller was glad he had written his request to the Senate. After all, there had been no naturalist aboard Spangberg's ships. On isolated islands, and in the seas surrounding them, a collector might well find endemic species—plants or animals unique to the place.

When Spangberg and Steller arrived in Okhotsk, they found Bering almost ready to sail for Kamchatka. The Captain Commander's adoring wife and two young children would soon be leaving in sedan chairs for St. Petersburg.

Bering was required by the Senate to take a mineralogist on his expeditions to Kamchatka and America so that valuable minerals might be identified, even when embedded in worthless rock. He invited Steller to come as far as Kamchatka in this role, and Steller accepted, hoping that he could eventually continue on to America with Bering. And he still had hopes of sailing to Japan with Spangberg, whose ships would not be outfitted and ready to leave for another year.

Spangberg had expected to be able to use the *Nadezhda* on his next expedition. But Bering, unaware of Spangberg's new orders, had already packed the ship with provisions for his time in Kamchatka. The winter freeze would make it impossible for the *Nadezhda* to return to Okhotsk before the spring of 1741.

8

The Volcanic Wilderness of Kamchatka

1740–1741

B ERING WAS IN HASTE TO LEAVE OKHOTSK BEFORE THE winter ice blocked the harbor, but an unexpected courier from the Senate demanding a complete plan for the voyage to America postponed his departure. On September 1, 1740, he ordered Master Sofron Khitrov, who would be his third-in-command on the *St. Peter*, to sail to Kamchatka in the *Nadezhda* as an advance party, carrying provisions for their year on the peninsula and for the voyage to America. But the ship did not reach the open sea; she ran aground on a sandbar before leaving the Okhotsk harbor. Some of the ship's biscuit and other irreplaceable provisions were lost in this first of many calamities caused by Khitrov's poor judgment. Lieutenant Sven Waxell, Bering's second-in-command and the only officer to write an eyewitness account of the voyage, protected his friend Khitrov by not mentioning this incident in his report. We learn of the event from Steller's journal.

The *Nadezhda* was repaired, and on September 8 she set sail again for Kamchatka, this time with Bering and his three ships, the

St. Peter, the *St. Paul*, and the *Okhotsk*, recently built for the government. Steller sailed on the *Okhotsk*, while Professor Louis de l'Isle de la Croyère, the French astronomer, sailed on the *St. Paul* under Captain Aleksei Chirikov. Bering commanded the *St. Peter*.

Two weeks later they reached Kamchatka's nearest harbor, Bolsheretsk, where Steller met Krasheninnikov for the first time. Although Krasheninnikov had spent three years leading the Kamchatka expedition, he had never been raised above the rank and salary of student. With the superior status of adjunct, Steller took charge immediately. Krasheninnikov gave Steller his excellent Russian hunter and servant, Toma Lopekhin, whom Steller regularly refers to in his journal as "my Cossack."

Steller helped Krasheninnikov pack and seal his extensive collections, which were then sent to Professor Gmelin by the next packet boat from Bolsheretsk.

While Steller, de la Croyère, and their assistants sailed on the *Okhotsk* up the Bolshaya River, exploring and making charts, the rest of Bering's flotilla—the *St. Peter*, the *St. Paul*, and the *Nadezhda*—set off on the dangerous course to the beautiful new harbor of Avacha Bay.

The *St. Peter* and the *St. Paul* arrived safely, but Khitrov nearly capsized the *Nadezhda* off treacherous Cape Lopatka and had to return to Bolsheretsk. There he ordered hundreds of Itelmen to carry his ship's cargo in dogsleds or on their backs over snow-covered volcanic mountains to Avacha Bay. Most of the Itelmen had never been separated from their families; some were taken from their homes three hundred miles away. Although they were paid for their services, money was meaningless to them, living as they did in a society in which goods were shared. Here again, Waxell, in his account, does not mention Khitrov's near disaster at Cape Lopatka and presents the decision to haul the provisions overland as one that had been made long before, in Okhotsk. The truth lay concealed in Steller's journal until it was published many years later.

Winter travel in Kamchatka was less predictable than in Siberia, where one could rely on the rivers freezing into a solid pavement from November to May. In Kamchatka, underwater hot springs melted sections of the frozen rivers or kept some rivers open all year round. Dogsleds and snowshoes were Steller's chief modes of travel in Kamchatka. There were no horses on the peninsula, and he does not mention using reindeer for transportation, although they were used by the Chukchis in the north. In the *History of Kamchatka*, a compilation of Steller's writings published some thirty years after his death, Steller explains the benefits and hardships of traveling by dogsled:

The sleds are engineered so well that the best mechanic could not have devised them any better. They seem to have their basis in the anatomy and structure of the human body . . . Although

everything on these sleds is very thin and supple, they nevertheless can endure truly amazing force. One often runs against trees in such a way that the sleds almost bend in half, without, however, sustaining the slightest damage . . . One sits on [the sled] mostly to one side, in order to be able to jump off right away at a dangerous spot.

Even though the journey with dogs is very difficult and dangerous and almost wears you out more than walking—you become dog-tired driving and traveling with dogs—dogsleds still have the advantage that you can travel with them . . . over impassable terrain where you could neither travel with horses nor, because of the deep snow, on foot. In addition to pulling, the dogs are good pathfinders and know how to find their way home in storms so bad a person cannot even open his eyes. If the storm is so fierce that one has to stop, which very frequently happens, the dogs lie down quietly and still beside their master for an hour or two, keeping him warm . . . Before a storm a person always gets a certain warning from the dogs about approaching bad weather because, if, during a rest stop, the dogs dig holes in the snow and lie down in them, then a person should certainly look

for a place where he can find shelter from the storm . . . The Cossacks call this *pogodi otlezhat'sia*, i.e., relaxing or lying down because of the weather, which is very commonplace.

For nine months Steller lived among the Itelmen, traveling with his interpreter from one settlement to another. He was amused by the Itelmen's impromptu theatrical performances, in which they brilliantly mimicked birds, animals, and people. Describing one entertainment, he wrote: "They imitate Captain Spangberg in the process of commanding all sails, using proper nautical terms, as well as my investigating and recording their manners and customs, with one of them acting the interpreter." Like Gmelin, his native hosts had seen that Steller was as meticulous in his scholarship as he was careless in his dress.

Steller applied his scientific approach to every aspect of Itelmen life. He was not content to observe that the men were polygamous and the women promiscuous and leave it at that. Steller learned that the Itelmen were tolerant of all kinds of sexual relationships. Sometimes a man dressed as a woman would join a household in the role of second wife, performing all the tasks usually performed by women and socially accepted as such. Steller noticed that Itelmen courtship practices, during which the would-be husband becomes a virtual slave in the house of his intended bride, firmly established the woman's ruling position in the relationship. A bride's parents were thought careless of her education if she was still a virgin by the time she married. Such a state was considered most undesirable; the skill gained from previous lovers was thought to enhance the pleasures of the wedding night.

We know from Gmelin's description that Steller was a remarkably self-sufficient traveler. Certain of his statements suggest a personal experience with local customs:

Whoever comes to Kamchatka and does not acquire a woman or live in secret understanding with another's wife is forced to do so from necessity. No one washes or sews for him, takes care of him or does him any favors unless he pays with sexual intercourse.

Bering wrote of the Itelmen, "A small number of these people are idolaters. The others do not believe in anything and are strangers to all good customs." Steller vehemently disagreed. He felt only admiration for these brilliant naturalists. The admiration seems to have been mutual. Steller notes, in a rare display of pride, that the Itelmen were amazed that he understood the fish of Kamchatka as well as they did. He identified five species of salmon alone and was the first European to grasp their complicated migratory life cycles.

Steller's careful attention to every aspect of Itelmen life, especially his mastery of the construction of their homes, would prove useful when he was shipwrecked on his way back from America. The Itelmen moved seasonally between communal underground dwellings and single-family homes that were raised off the ground on stilts. Their unusual villages were perfectly adapted to the long, cold winters and the wet summers.

They liked to settle close to lakes or to places where small streams emptied into larger rivers, and where there were lots of trees or bushes. No matter how few people live in the village or how small the individual dwellings are, all the villages look very large and imposing because of the separate winter and summer dwellings as well as *ambars* [storehouses].

At the beginning of November, they move into their winter dwellings, where they stay until the beginning of April . . . The only way to get into the dwelling is to climb in through the smoke hole down a ladder or a tree into which steps have been hewn. As difficult as this seems for a European, especially when a fire is burning and he nearly suffocates from the smoke, it is quite easy for the Itelmen as a matter of habit . . . When the snow and earth thaw . . . the underground dwellings fill with water, and the inhabitants then retreat into the summer dwellings or balagans, which stand up in the air on poles like dovecotes . . .

Each family . . . has its separate balagan because it is easier to build and maintain than the winter dwellings and does not require lighting or heating . . . The balagans are . . . built like pyramids . . . standing on nine to twelve posts secured with thongs. The upper structure consists of poles that are tied together at the top and covered entirely with straw . . . These balagans are built

so close together that a person can get from one to another on bridges or planks . . . These birdhouses are also occasionally blown over by the wind. People who live in balagans for the first time get dizzy because balagans rock constantly like cradles, especially in strong winds . . .

The inhabitants dry fish under

the balagans where the air, but not the moisture, can get at them. People also dry their nettles, roots, and herbs and store their sleds and other equipment under the balagans. The dogs are tied to the balagan posts, which is the only shelter the dogs need.

In his journal, Steller drew upon a range of images and experiences from his childhood to describe the plants and animals of Kamchatka. Sleeping cormorants nestling close together as they perch against a cliff face remind him of apothecary jars arranged on a pharmacist's shelf; a birdcall evokes the sound of the toy trumpets sold to children at the renowned Nuremberg Christmas fair.

As a scientist, Steller naturally noted the appearance, habitat, and behavior of Kamchatka's many unusual birds, but he also observed their religious and cultural significance. Biology and fashion merge in his descriptions of the puffins of Kamchatka.

HORNED PUFFIN

The horned puffin looks like and is the size of a duck. The part of its body projecting above water while swimming is entirely black; the rest is white. The most remarkable thing about it is its large, wide, parrot-like vermilion beak . . . The inhabitants tie their beaks on strings or cords, interspersed with little dyed bundles of seal hair. These cords, previously made by the female shamans, were hung around everyone's neck and worn on the bare chest as good luck necklaces, as nowadays the cross is.

Tufted Puffin

The tufted puffin . . . has two unique yellowish-white long feather tufts hanging toward the nape of its neck on both sides of its head, which look very pretty . . . Itelmen women who want to look very elegant wear two hand-sized pieces of white wolverine fur on their heads above the ears . . . Thus they imitate the two tufts of whitish-yellow feathers on this bird's head.

Steller united his love of music and natural history when he described the duck called the old squaw. Did its song and Itelmen name remind him of singing in the choir as a boy in Windsheim?

Old Squaw Duck

The old squaw . . . has a very curious call, always sounding six notes in the same sequence.

Because these birds always stay together in flocks, their combined calls create the most amazing varied harmonies. This

duck's internal ear is shaped like a rattle fife, also having three holes that are covered with a very thin membrane inside, through which these various tones are so accurately formed. The Itelmen have special poems about this duck and have composed melodies, which cleverly imitate its call. The Itelmen call this duck *aan-gitsh*, which is what they also call the bell-ringer or church sexton because he produces different sounds with different bells and also ding-dongs bright and early during matins, like these ducks at daybreak.

Steller was impressed by the resourcefulness of the Itelmen. They were so self-sufficient and inventive, making such good use of their plants and animals, that they had little experience of trading with outside people. As a result, their Russian overlords easily took advantage of them, encouraging them to go into debt, then charging exorbitant interest to be paid in furs. But sometimes fur-bearing animals were scarce due to weather, predators, or overhunting. The Itelmen could not be sure that their catch would cover even the interest on their debt.

The Itelmen had adapted to the long, freezing winters; Steller noticed that they never complained of the cold. But they did suffer from snow blindness caused by the dazzling brightness of the snow, highly polished by the wind. The condition was aggravated by the smoky atmosphere inside their underground dwellings. In response, the Itelmen had invented sunglasses of a sort long before they were used in Europe.

Steller's detailed journal entries offer proof of their ingenuity:

EYE PROTECTORS

On Kamchatka the snow reflects the sun so fiercely in the spring that the people turn as black as American Indians, and their eyes become so irritated that many go blind. Even the healthiest eyes become so inflamed that they cannot bear the least bit of daylight, which is why the inhabitants wear eye protectors, i.e., nets of birch bark and horse hair over their eyes, allowing them to see through a narrow slit, which tempers and distributes the brightness of the rays.

GRASSES AND RAINCOATS

Along the ocean a tall grass grows whose stalk and head look similar to grain. The natives weave all sorts of mats from this grass . . . From this grass they also weave very attractive, serviceable raincoats that are smooth inside and shaggy on the outside, trimmed with a woven seam or border of straw. During the summer when it rains, they always wear these raincoats around their shoulders. And the coats perform as intended, so there is no danger of rain soaking through . . .

They cover over their summer and winter dwellings . . . with all types of long dried grass and in a short time can cut a large amount of grass with a bone sickle made from the shoulder blade of a bear which, with stones, they know how to make as sharp as an iron one.

Steller found the Itelmen women, who used such simple materials as cotton grass for many purposes, especially industrious and clever. Siberian tribes ignored the plant's possibilities.

COTTON GRASS

Out of *gramine Cyperoide*, or "Cypergrass," which elsewhere is not considered useful for anything, the natives card a type of soft grass, which looks like freshly carded flax, with a two-pronged comb made of seagull bones . . . Every year in autumn a very large supply of this grass is gathered for the following uses:

(1) When children are born, this grass serves to keep the child covered up and clean, in the absence of shirts and diapers.

(2) When the child grows up, this grass is used for stockings. They know how to wind it around their feet so cleverly that it stays on the foot like a legging. Everyone uses it when traveling because it is so soft, warm, and convenient.

(3) Until the children are "toilet trained," they wear pants which have a drop seat in the back in which grass is put. When the grass is dirtied, the mother just undoes the drop seat and the excrement falls out with the grass, and a fresh bunch of grass is placed in the child's pants . . .

(5) This grass is their tinder, from which they blow embers into flames.

(6) They used to bind this grass together like a garland around their heads during festivals, especially when a ball or dance was held.

(7) When a sacrifice is made or an animal is slaughtered and consumed, it receives a grass garland in exchange for its flesh, so

it will not be angry or complain to its relatives . . . [The people] also did the same thing to the enemies they killed.

SARANA

The term *sarana* was used to describe any of five bulbs and tubers used as a staple food by the Itelmen:

All of these bulbs are of great value to the Kamchadals; they are eaten raw and cooked with fish. Out of them the people make *pirogen* or pastries, called *salamat* in Russian because they are fried in fish fat. Every year they gather a large supply of bulbs, which they dry in the sun.

Besides harvesting sarana bulbs in the wild themselves, the Itelmen ceremoniously raided the nests of lemmings—Steller called them "mice"—who had laid in their own winter supply:

They take part of this supply from the mice with strange ceremonies and superstitions in the following way: In those years in which there are many mice, they also get a lot of sarana, which is the same to them as bread is to the Russians. When they dig up the mouse nest, it must be done with an instrument made out of reindeer antler, called *koscikoas*. While digging, they call all the things with different and strange names, which produces an entirely different language, so that the mice, who are said to understand the local language, cannot understand what is being said.

When they have taken out all the supply, never killing a mouse in the process, they put in old rags, broken needles, fire-

weed, cow parsnips, pine nuts and some sarana, intending it to look like a trade because they have given the mice clothes, beds, tools and other things. If they do not do this, they believe, the mice will drown or hang themselves, and consequently, the people will lose workers. They also ask the mice not to hold it against them, for they had not done it out of evil intent but out of friendship.

Up and down the Kamchatka Peninsula, Steller collected natural history specimens and interviewed native people. He knew that scurvy was the chief cause of death on long sea voyages and among men who spent the winter charting the Arctic coast. Thirteen of Spangberg's men had died of it, yet none of the native people were afflicted. As a doctor who would soon have the care of many sailors in his hands, Steller eagerly sought cures for the deadly condition from the Kamchadal female shamans, whom he held in high esteem. Perhaps in response to his deference, or because they recognized him as someone who also wished to understand nature, or simply because, as a doctor and botanist, he knew the questions to ask, the women showed him which plants to gather and how to prepare them.

Scurvy actually bothers only the new arrivals on Kamchatka, but the Cossack children and the Itelmen not at all because of their mixed diet of many roots, plants and tree bark, including wild garlic, called *cheremsha*, the yellow and black scurvy berries, called *moroshki* [cloudberry] and *shiksha* [crowberry], and frozen fish eaten raw . . . A decoction of scrub pine, called *slanets*, is very useful and obviously effective; also a decoction made from the buds of stone alder shrubs has an even greater effect and a very pleasant aroma.

Steller gratefully wrote this tribute to the native people of Kamchatka:

They . . . know the efficacy of all plants according to various places where they grow and the time to collect them, to such a degree that I could not admire them enough.

THE OTHER MYSTERY, BESIDES A CURE FOR SCURVY, WAS THE BEST route to America. Steller thought that even rumors were better than no information at all. He described his technique for extracting opinions, even from the unwilling:

I eagerly took pains to obtain such information, questioning all newcomers, traders, Cossacks with the greatest friendliness, and, in case I got nothing out of them with fair means, brought them to confession with brandy, as the most pleasant torture.

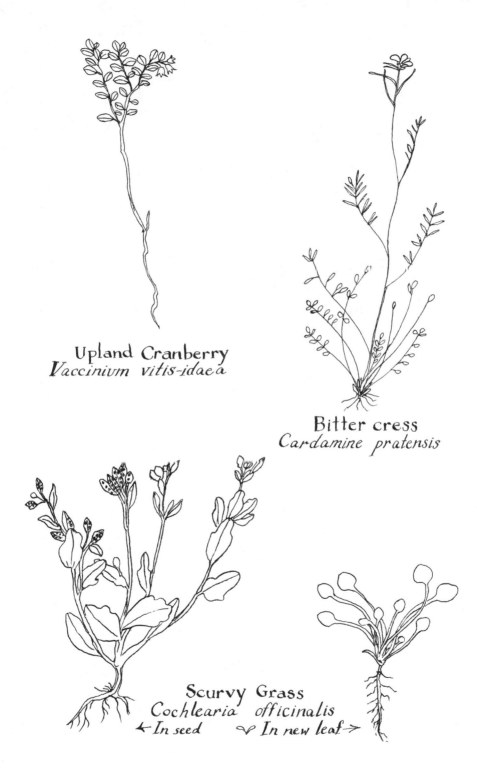

Upland Cranberry
Vaccinium vitis-idaea

Bitter cress
Cardamine pratensis

Scurvy Grass
Cochlearia officinalis
← *In seed*   ⩔ *In new leaf* →

9
Avacha Bay:
Steller Signs
On to the *St. Peter*
1741

I N FEBRUARY 1741, BERING SENT A MESSAGE TELLING STELLER to meet him on the other side of Kamchatka in the port of Petropavlovsk. The naturalist traveled ten days by dogsled to Avacha Bay. He arrived to learn that some of the Itelmen used by Khitrov to carry the contents of the *Nadezhda* overland had rebelled and murdered the Cossacks who had led this forced march. In consequence, and to set an example throughout Kamchatka, the rebels

had been rounded up and taken to Bering at Avacha Bay. Steller was shocked to see the cruel beatings meted out as punishment. Some of the natives had committed suicide out of despair. He confronted Bering, then secretly wrote to the Senate in St. Petersburg proposing a different way of treating the native people—schemes for agriculture, education, new settlements, and improved religious instruction. A year later, when Spangberg returned from Japan, he also petitioned the Senate to install a just governor in Kamchatka.

In Petropavlovsk, Steller presented Bering with the information he had gathered and his conclusion that America lay to the northeast, as indeed it did. But Bering dismissed Steller's evidence and responded, "People talk much; who would believe a Cossack? I place no confidence whatsoever in it."

In spite of his objection to Steller's sources of information, Bering was nonetheless impressed with Steller's abilities. The Captain Commander was satisfied with the way Steller had carried out his work in Kamchatka; now he invited him to share his cabin on the *St. Peter* as mineralogist. This was Steller's title on the roster of men on board, but Bering needed him to serve in other capacities as well. The ship's doctor had recently fallen ill and asked to return to St. Petersburg, leaving only an assistant surgeon, Matthias Betge, to look after seventy-eight men. There was no naturalist or Lutheran minister on board. While Steller had never been ordained, he had studied theology as well as medicine in Wittenberg and Halle. Bering found in Steller a man who could perform all of these roles. Steller hesitated. He worried about changing his plans after asking the Senate for permission to go to Japan with Captain Spangberg; also, he needed an artist to record his ethnographical and natural history discoveries. He himself did not draw and he had left his student assistant, Gorlanov, and his artist, Berckhan, in Bolsheretsk to carry out explorations and paint specimens. Bering assured him that as Captain Commander he had the authority to select Steller for the appointment; it could be viewed as an extension of the Kam-

chatka assignment. When Bering introduced him to Friedrich Plenisner, who would come along as surveyor and artist, Steller gladly agreed to sail for America.

The Admiralty's instructions had been to build two warships, complete with cannons, gunpowder, and a medicine cabinet full of salves and bandages. But no provision had been made against scurvy or asthma, the two chief medical complaints on long sea voyages. Steller, as the ship's doctor, criticized these arrangements from the beginning, but Bering ignored his advice.

In case of a naval battle, there were sixteen soldiers, five grenadiers, and four gunners on board Bering's ship. The other members of the *St. Peter*'s crew consisted of a blacksmith, a sailmaker, two coopers (who made and repaired barrels), a caulker, four carpenters, fourteen sailors, a purser, a midshipman, a boatswain and his two helpers, and Bering's personal attendants. Three natives of Kamchatka came along to act as interpreters. Captain Chirikov, in the *St. Paul*, had a crew of similar composition, but only his navigator, Ivan Yelagin, who had been in charge of building the town of Petropavlovsk before Bering's arrival, was qualified to record entries in the ship's log. There is no native interpreter listed on the roster of the *St. Paul*, but in his account of the voyage Chirikov does mention a Kodiak interpreter. There were no trumpeters on board, but they had a monk.

The *St. Peter*'s officers, who would serve as members of a sea council, were:

Vitus Jonassen Bering, Captain Commander. Danish. His immediate staff consisted of two trumpeters and a drummer to announce his embarking or disembarking from the ship; an assistant, Dmitri Ovtsin; and two personal servants. German was his household language.

Sven Waxell, First Lieutenant. Swedish. Guided by Bering, he took care of the everyday running of the ship in preparation for becoming a captain himself one day. He volunteered for the expedition in 1733, at the age of thirty-one, and was the only crew member to have been with Bering from the beginning of the Second Kamchatka Expedition.

Sofron Khitrov, Lieutenant. Russian. Khitrov left Okhotsk under a cloud of mystery. Whether Bering hired him to bring a Russian into a position of command or out of kindness, in hopes of restoring Khitrov's reputation, is unknown. With the help of Waxell, Khitrov kept one of the two ship's logs. (Steller's journal and Khitrov's log entries vary significantly at some crucial moments of the expedition.)

Andreas Hesselberg, first mate. To judge by his name, Hesselberg was probably either Danish or German. He was almost seventy years old and had been at sea for fifty years. Steller admired and respected his knowledge and experience.

Kharlam Yushin, assistant navigator. Russian. He kept the ship's second log with the help of Andreas Hesselberg.

Dmitri Ovtsin, seaman. Russian. In 1734, as a lieutenant, Ovtsin had commanded the two-masted shallop *Tobol*, surveying the Ob River and the western Siberian coastline on the Kara Sea. He would have been in Waxell's position on the voyage to America if he had not been demoted to the rank of ordinary seaman as punishment for befriending an exiled Russian prince in Siberia. Bering chose to overlook this episode when he selected Ovtsin as his assistant. It was only after returning to Kamchatka that Ovtsin discovered that his rank of lieutenant had been restored to him in February 1741.

The only child on board was Laurentz Waxell, the eleven-year-old son of Lieutenant Waxell.

Georg Steller was the sole representative of the Academy of Sciences on the *St. Peter*.

PETER THE GREAT HAD SET AN EXAMPLE FOR HIS COUNTRYMEN by working his way up through the naval ranks. He insisted that his officers go through the same rigorous training. In the meantime, for want of qualified Russians, many captains and officers in the Russian Imperial Navy were foreigners. In an attempt to increase Russian representation, or prevent foreign domination, the Admiralty required a captain to consult all the officers in a ship's council before making an important decision. Under dire circumstances everyone on board, regardless of rank, joined in the discussion and signed his name to the agreement. It was natural for Bering to assign two Russians to keep the *St. Peter*'s logbooks, written in Cyrillic script. While the foreigners who assisted Yushin and Khitrov in this task were more experienced as sailors, they were probably less fluent in writing Russian. Bering may also have been protecting himself against criticism from the Admiralty when he gave this responsibility to the highest-ranking Russians on board. On his voyage to Japan, Spangberg did the same, putting Matvej Petrov in charge of the logbook.

In Petropavlovsk, Bering held a sea council of the officers of the

St. Peter and the *St. Paul* to decide the ships' course, the duration of the voyage, and the signals to be given between the two ships. Steller was not invited to this meeting because the astronomer Professor de la Croyère, sailing under Captain Chirikov on the *St. Paul*, represented the Academy of Sciences. De la Croyère insisted that they use a map drawn by his half brother the famous astronomer and geographer Joseph Nicolas Delisle, who had arranged for de la Croyère to join the expedition. The map depicted a large, unconfirmed landmass labeled "Juan de Gama Land," which was to be their first destination.

Originally, the Admiralty had authorized a two-year voyage, allowing for overwintering in America. As a result of Khitrov's earlier accident aboard the *Nadezhda* in Okhotsk harbor, the food supply on the ships was much less than had been planned. The officers had no choice but to go to America and back in a single sailing season—from late May to September.

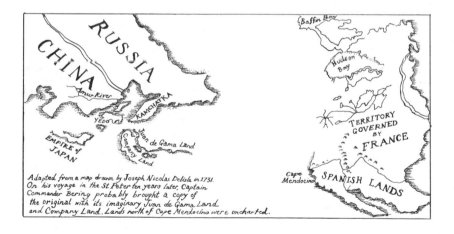

Adapted from a map drawn by Joseph Nicolas Delisle in 1731. On his voyage in the St. Peter ten years later, Captain Commander Bering probably brought a copy of the original with its imaginary Juan de Gama Land and Company Land. Lands north of Cape Mendocino were uncharted.

10
They Set Sail
for America
JUNE 1741

ON JUNE 4, 1741, THE *ST. PETER* UNDER CAPTAIN COMMAN-
der Bering and the *St. Paul* under Captain Chirikov set sail
from Avacha Bay intending to stay together throughout the voyage,
in case either ship needed help. The captains had agreed upon a
code of flags and cannon fire to signal a change of course or desire
for conversation. Two weeks later, however, the ships lost each other
in the night. The two crews did not meet again until the end of the
voyage.

When the *St. Peter* reached the longitude and latitude for "Juan
de Gama Land," the sea stretched before them and land was
nowhere to be seen. Joseph Nicolas Delisle's map had led them
astray, and they had no other map to consult. Steller thought that
his knowledge of seabirds and seaweeds and their usual proximity
to land should direct their course, while the sailors thought that
their years of seagoing experience entitled them to reject his advice.
Sometimes Steller was correct, but not always. Early in the voyage,
Bering had sailed south for four days following Steller's recommen-

dation. When no land was sighted, Bering returned to the course decided upon at the Petropavlovsk sea council, and from then on took no notice of Steller's observations.

For six weeks they roamed the Pacific Ocean in an easterly direction, bickering about where America might lie. Steller wrote in his journal, "No matter what we observed . . . the answer was always ready: 'You do not understand it; you are not a seaman.' "

Steller was the first to sight land on July 15, but a bank of clouds rapidly obscured it, and nobody believed him. The next day, however, the mountains of the mainland rose up dramatically before them out of the clouds and mist. There was an island in the foreground. Everyone hoped they had reached America.

They had discovered Alaska, but Bering was not elated. Steller wrote in his journal:

It can easily be imagined how happy every one was when land was finally sighted; nobody failed to congratulate the Captain Commander . . . but in the presence of all he even shrugged his shoulders while looking at the land . . . [Later] in the cabin he expressed himself to me and Mr. Plenisner as follows: "We think now we have accomplished everything, and many go about greatly inflated, but they do not consider where we have reached land, how far we are from home, and what may yet happen; who knows but that perhaps trade winds may arise, which may prevent us from returning? We do not know this country; nor are we provided with supplies for a wintering."

In his final report, Waxell wrote of Bering:

It was one of his favourite sayings that there is no art in sending people off on a journey, for that was something they were accustomed to manage by themselves, but that to find them subsistence when they reached their destination was a thing that called for considerably more prudence and thought.

They chose a large island close to the Alaskan mainland as their landing site and named it St. Elias after the saint commemorated on the day they came ashore. They also named its southern cape Cape St. Elias. The island is now known as Kayak Island, but the cape retains the saint's name.

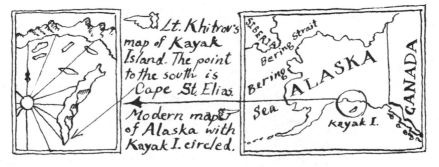

Lt. Khitrov's map of Kayak Island. The point to the south is Cape St. Elias.

Modern map of Alaska with Kayak I. circled.

Although Bering allowed Khitrov to go in the longboat to look for a safe anchorage, he would not give Steller permission to land. This brought out the sarcasm in Steller's temperament, which, after the annoyances of the voyage, cannot have been far from the surface. He wrote in his journal:

> Only on one point were all unanimous, viz. that we should take fresh water on board, so that I could not help saying that we had come only for the purpose of bringing American water to Asia. It was agreed, besides, that the small yawl should be used for the transportation of the water, while the larger should be given to Master Khitrov with a sufficient crew and ammunition in order that he might explore the country, a task for which he possessed the best qualifications . . .
>
> When I asked to be sent off at the same time as Master Khitrov since he did not, after all, know everything (Khitrov himself, knowing his strengths, also asked for my company), our request was denied, and at first the attempt was made to scare me with some gruesome murder stories.
>
> But I answered that I had never acted like a woman, nor did I know any reason why I should not be permitted to go ashore. To get there was, after all, to follow my chief work, profession, and duty. Up to now I had served Her Majesty faithfully according to my ability and was willing to maintain the honor of my service for a long time yet. And I said that if for reasons contrary to the purpose of the voyage I was not to go, I would report such conduct in terms it deserved.
>
> I was then called a wild man who would not be kept from work even by a treat to chocolate, which was just then being prepared.

Steller was resigned to hearing that he would never be a sailor, but to be told that he could not even be a naturalist infuriated him.

Was Bering afraid of losing his doctor and minister in the wilderness of the island? Was he trying to thwart Steller's ambitions? Or was he only teasing, perhaps wishing Steller would take himself less seriously, all the while intending to let him go ashore? If so, Bering did not understand that the study of mankind and the natural world was something that Steller could not take lightly. He had waited all his life for this opportunity.

The next day Steller prevailed.

On my departure from the ship, the Captain Commander attempted to find out if I could take a joke by having trumpets sounded after me. Without thanking him, I took the matter the way it had been ordered. But I have never been one to blow my own horn and would not have appreciated it if trumpets had been sounded in my honor . . .

I had gone scarcely one verst [a little more than half a mile] along the coast before I found in one spot signs of people and what they were like. Under a tree I found an old piece of log hewn as a trough in which a few hours earlier the savages, lacking

kettles and dishes, had cooked meat with glowing stones according to Kamchatkan ways described elsewhere. Where they had been sitting, bones lay scattered, some with meat remaining, that had the appearance of having been roasted at the fire . . . I likewise found lying in various shells, as in bowls, sweet grass over which water had previously been poured in order to extract the sweetness, which struck me as quite remarkable and led me to the following conclusions.

This rare grass was up to now thought to be unique to the Kamchadals . . . The way of preparing it by cleaning the outer part with clamshells, as well as the way in which it is eaten, corresponds exactly with American practice. On the other hand, this custom is unknown to the neighboring Tungus and Olenni Koriaks living in Kamchatka.

They came to a spot covered with cut grass. Hidden beneath layers of grass, rocks, and tree bark was a cellar full of winter provisions, hunting weapons, and fishing gear. There were containers over a yard high, made of tree bark and filled with smoked salmon. When he found the dried inner bark from larch or spruce trees done up in rolls, Steller recognized the food used in time of famine in Kamchatka, Siberia, and eastern Russia.

Steller's knowledge of the Kamchadal foodstuffs and food

preparation made him suspect that these Americans, Eskimos of the Ugalakmiut tribe, had originally come from Kamchatka. But he was waiting for further evidence; he wanted to meet the people themselves.

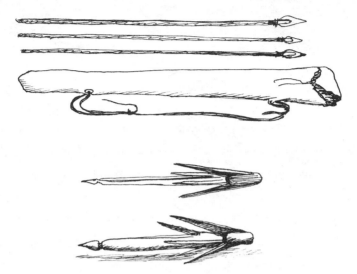

Steller sent Toma, his Siberian servant, back to the ship with samples of native products from the cellar. He wanted Toma to give the samples to Bering and to convey a request for two or three men to help him investigate the island. He then covered over the cellar and walked alone into the wooded hills to get a view of the mainland in the distance. In just one day he had discovered many plants and birds unknown to science. Steller reflected that they could have overwintered in America if only Khitrov had not lost so much of their food in the Okhotsk harbor.

He returned to the beach, laden with specimens, to find the watering party loading the last barrels onto the yawl. Again Steller sent a request to the ship for a few men to help him.

Dead tired, I made in the meantime descriptions on the beach of the rarer plants which I was afraid might wither and was delighted to be able to test out the excellent water for tea.

He described 144 plants in Latin. Among his discoveries was a native raspberry. Although the fruit was not yet ripe, it promised to be large and delicious. Steller planted several specimens in wooden boxes and insisted on bringing them aboard ship.

During the eight and a half Siberian years of the expedition the Admiralty and Academy contingents had spent long periods apart, their orders arriving from different official bodies. When they met, there was always friction between the two groups, sometimes over resources, but also over the value and importance of their respective work. Did aspects of this rivalry color Bering's relations with Steller, who was, after all, an academic? So far as we know, only his draftsman, Plenisner, and his servant, Toma, in any way shared Steller's interest in natural history. No one else on board took his request for help seriously. They were blind to the value of having a great naturalist direct the investigation of a country totally unknown to Europeans. Instead, there was a general feeling that Steller's collections, and Steller himself, uselessly cluttered the ship.

As evening was already nearing, I sent my Cossack out to shoot some rare birds that I had noticed . . . Good luck, thanks to my huntsman, placed in my hands a single specimen, of which I remember to have seen a likeness painted in lively colors and de-

scribed in the newest account of the birds and plants of the Car-
olinas . . . This bird proved to me that we were really in America.

Today we know it as Steller's jay.

Bering sent a reply to Steller's request for help; he must return
to the ship at once or risk being left behind. Knowing he had
stayed away too long, Steller dreaded meeting his captain. At the
same time he was angry with Bering for not sending men to help
him.

But when Steller arrived, instead of chastisement, a surprise
reception awaited him. Bering
handed him a cup of rare and precious hot chocolate. The cocoa had
been brought from the far coast of
South America all the way to St.
Petersburg, and from there across
Siberia to serve in celebration of
reaching this other distant coast of the New World.

Bering, standing on the deck, had lost sight of Steller as he
walked through the more forested parts of the island. He was probably quite relieved to have his doctor back on board.

Steller couldn't resist showing his finds and suggesting that
gifts replace what he had taken from the native cellar. He took no
part, however, in choosing the presents.

An iron kettle, a pound of tobacco, a Chinese pipe, and a
piece of Chinese silk were sent to the cellar, but in return the lat-
ter was plundered to such an extent that, if we should come again

to these parts, the natives would certainly run away even faster or they would show themselves as hostile as they themselves had been treated, especially if it should occur to them to eat or drink the tobacco . . . A couple of knives or hatchets . . . would have aroused the interest of these savages much more.

Unbeknownst to Steller—as we learn from the ship's logs—knives *had* in fact been left as presents.

Bering had ordered his men to bring him all of the excellent smoked salmon from the native cellar. No doubt it made a delicious addition to the captain's table. But Steller did not approve of stealing the food supply. He knew that the preserved fish could save the natives from starvation during the severe northern winter. Looking into the future, he saw that the Russians would be hated and feared for such deeds. Steller's attitude, however, was most unusual in

eighteenth-century Russia. At a time when contact between Europeans and native peoples was marked by exploitation, religious conversion, or curiosity, Steller's outrage must have seemed quite unreasonable to Bering.

The next morning the Captain Commander did as he pleased.

July 21, 1741

> Two hours before daybreak, the Captain Commander . . . without
> consulting anyone, gave orders to weigh anchor . . . It was con-
> sidered reason enough that the wind just then blew favorably for
> getting out and contrary for going into the harbor.

Steller saw his chance for further investigation disappear as the
ship pulled away from the land. He fervently wished they could
overwinter on the mainland, meet the native people, and record the
flora and fauna scientifically. In his frustration he wrote:

> The time here spent in investigation bears an arithmetical ratio
> to the time used in fitting out: ten years the preparations for this
> great undertaking lasted, and ten hours were devoted to the work
> itself.

But Bering knew how dangerous the sea could become, especially as the seasons changed. He was acting responsibly, just as he
had on the First Kamchatka Expedition. The daylight hours were
already getting shorter, and a storm could strike at any time, day or
night, and drive them against an unseen rocky coast.

As Captain Commander, Bering surely felt answerable for the
safe return of every man on his ship. With a family of four children,
a loving, devoted wife, and hopes of finally being rewarded with a
country estate, he saw no reason to linger in Alaska. Science, on the
other hand, was Steller's great passion. It was his sole motive for
joining the expedition; he was willing to risk his life for it. Four
years after his departure from St. Petersburg, his feelings for his
wife had become ambivalent. In his letters to Gmelin, Steller
grumbled that Brigitta Helena devoted her correspondence to requests for money rather than expressions of sympathy for his situation. She would not accompany him to Siberia and yet received half

his salary. Bering was naturally as avid to return home as Steller was to continue his explorations. It cannot have been easy for two men of such diverse inclinations to share a cabin.

Steller was not the only one to object to Bering's plans. Knowing that the winds would be against them on their return voyage, Bering wanted to hasten back along the familiar route he had charted on his way to America. But Officers Khitrov and Waxell, justified by the laws of the Russian Navy, overruled their commander. They insisted on carrying out the plan that had been decided upon two and a half months earlier in Bolsheretsk, that is, following whatever uncharted land extended from America on the return voyage. In fact, this meant the dangerous mapping of the arc of the Aleutian Islands and sailing back twice as many miles as on their journey out. Bering's judgment was superior to that of his lower officers, but he had to yield to their majority decision.

11
Return Voyage: Kayaks and Death
JULY–SEPTEMBER 1741

NOT LONG AFTER THE SHIP LEFT THE ISLAND, AFFAIRS ON board the *St. Peter* took a frightening turn for the worse. One by one the officers and crew were succumbing to scurvy; everyone knew it was only a matter of time before the disease would grip the entire vessel. Whether the crew was healthy or sick, the same amount of work had to be done, and the healthier crew members had to do it all. They climbed up into the rigging to set the sails, tried to navigate toward Kamchatka, and maintained the ship as best they could by repairing the rigging and mending the sails before they were reduced to threads and rags. The healthy men had to extend their watches—the exhausting task of peering through fog, sleet, or snow in uncharted waters—trying to discern a rock or even an island looming up out of the rain or darkness somewhere in front of them.

Meanwhile, those who were ill lay in their hammocks day and night with no one to bring them a bedpan. The stench from the hold was horrendous; it permeated the ship.

As the men struggled with declining health, Steller's journal entries record the advent of the autumn storms, which gave further reason to fear the voyage home.

July 28–29

Continuous stormy and wet weather.

August 3–9

We saw large numbers of hair seals, sea otters, fur seals, sea lions, . . . dolphins, and storm fishes [porpoises] . . . Whenever these animals were to be seen unusually often in a very quiet sea, a storm followed soon after; and . . . the oftener they came up and the more active they were, the more furious was the subsequent gale.

August 20–23

I saw at this time whales very frequently, no longer singly but in pairs, swimming together side by side or pursuing one another, which made me think that this must be their mating time.

By the end of August, Lieutenant Waxell was making many of the ship's decisions, only occasionally referring a question to Captain Commander Bering, who had been bedridden for three weeks and could not move his arms or legs. At least twelve members of the crew were also now suffering from symptoms of scurvy. They were acutely sensitive to loud noises, and their gums were swollen and painful, increasing their depression and lethargy. Steller was the only man on board who knew how to combat the disease; he had learned from the Kamchadal women shamans which plants could cure the men.

On August 29, the *St. Peter* came upon a cluster of islands and found safe harbor within their circle.

Waxell sent Khitrov with several men, including a Chukchi interpreter, to one of the islands in the yawl to investigate a beach where fire had been noticed on the previous night, with instructions to return as soon as possible.

Steller went ashore in the longboat with the water carriers under the old pilot Andreas Hesselberg. Later he wrote:

> I was scarcely ashore when I immediately endeavored to locate a watering place and found several springs with very good and safe water, but at the same time the seamen had selected the first and nearest puddle and already begun the transport. However, I noted the following flaws in this water: namely, (1) that it was standing, chalky water, which I recognized right away by boiling tea and then by testing with soap; and (2) that, as I had observed on the beach, it rose and fell with the tide and therefore shared its salt, which immediately became apparent during boiling, unless one had totally lost one's taste.
>
> I thus proposed to use the spring water I had found, of which I sent a sample to the ship together with an oral report, which besides information on the quality of the water contained the following: that by using the other water, scurvy would quickly increase, and because of its lime, the men would be dried up and debilitated, indeed, that this water after a short time aboard ship would increase in salinity from day to day and through standing finally become salt water. On the other hand, there was nothing of the sort to be feared from the spring water.

Imagine Steller's indignation when Hesselberg returned with the brackish water and delivered Waxell's stubborn reply, "Why, what is the matter with this water? The water is good, fill up with it!" It was a fatal decision.

There was no point in arguing with Hesselberg, who had to abide by Waxell's choice, so Steller left him and set off to explore the island.

The next day Steller was thwarted again when he found herbs to combat scurvy and needed help in gathering them.

[We] found here . . . the glorious antiscorbutic herbs, such as *Cochlearia, Lapathum folio cubitali, Gentiana* and other cresslike herbs, which I gathered . . . I . . . requested the detail of several men for the purpose of collecting . . . enough for all, nevertheless even this proposition . . . was spurned.

At this time Waxell believed that no one really knew the cause of scurvy or its cure. Following Bering's lead on Kayak Island, he may have felt Steller was being unreasonable and frivolous in suggesting that crew members pick plants. Waxell was unwilling to assign anyone to the task. He did, however, allow the sailors suffering from scurvy to be brought ashore in hopes that the fresh air and quiet would restore their health.

Steller spent this day with Plenisner exploring the island while eating and gathering plants. They probably shared their discoveries with Betge, the assistant surgeon, and Toma when they returned to the ship with herbs, crowberries, and lingonberries.

Steller built a little hut on the misty island, intending to spend the night there observing nature. But his concern for the crew brought him back to the ship that evening, where he tried to convince Waxell that freshwater and herbs were essential for restoring the men's health. He was rudely informed that the water was fine and he could gather the herbs himself.

However, a lamentable event on the next day made even Waxell uncomfortable with his decision.

AUGUST 31

On this day we buried the first of our crew, the sailor Shumagin, who had died on the previous day almost as soon as he got ashore.

A Russian cross was placed over the grave both to mark its location and to claim the islands for the Russian Empire. They were later named the Shumagin Islands.

After Nikita Shumagin's death, Lieutenant Waxell regretted choosing the brackish water. He sent ten empty barrels ashore to be filled at Steller's source, intending to use them for the officers. But when the wind came up, the barrels had to be left behind. Furious that his advice as ship's doctor had been ignored, Steller considered it to be divine justice.

> Towards evening, we were hurriedly called on board . . . because of an apprehended storm . . . All the men were being assembled . . . in case the anchors did not hold in the rising gale.

Waxell had told Khitrov to return to the ship as soon as possible in case of the sudden appearance of foul weather. The *St. Peter* would have sailed immediately, for the wind was favorable. Indeed, at that very moment the wind was filling the sails of her sister ship, the *St. Paul*, making her way swiftly back to Kamchatka. But Khitrov had not returned, and they could not leave without him. At night they could see from the ship his huge bonfire on the shore; he had reached the watering island but could go no farther. Khitrov's boat had crashed onto the rocky beach and was too badly damaged to row back to the ship.

Five days later, when the strong fair wind toward Kamchatka— which made it impossible to reach Khitrov's party—had blown itself out, Waxell was at last able to send the longboat to retrieve Khitrov and his men from the island, where they abandoned the battered yawl.

As he reached the ship, Khitrov took the lead in his hand to measure the depth of the harbor,

> and at the first attempt left it on the bottom of the sea, which incident the common sailors interpreted as an evil omen and called to mind that just a year ago today the provisions were lost at the mouth of the Okhota River through this same man's cleverness.

As the sailors became ever more confirmed in their low opinion of Khitrov and his actions, their assessment of Steller and his abilities underwent a dramatic change. To the sailors' surprise, Steller's cures for scurvy began to work—and very quickly, too.

September 5

The *Lapathum* I prescribed to be eaten raw for three days firmed up again the teeth of most seamen.

As the captain and his men recovered their health, Steller's status aboard ship altered forever. He was no longer the crackpot naturalist trying to find land by means of seaweeds or the fool who brought on board bundles of herbs and raspberry plants needing attention. Men whose teeth were about to fall out could now eat without pain, and even the captain was gaining strength. It seemed almost miraculous. From then on he was addressed as "Dr. Steller"—without sarcasm.

But the naturalist dreaded the results of everyone drinking bad water and feared that the supply of herbs on board was too small. He could not forgive Waxell's stubborn refusal to listen to his sensible advice. Not that Waxell asked his forgiveness or expressed remorse of any kind—in his report to the Senate, he claimed that both water samples were brackish and that the crew had spent all night refilling the water barrels in haste to leave the island before a storm. Neither statement was true; nor did he mention that he had acted against the recommendations of the ship's doctor.

They spent the day trying to reach the open sea, but now the direction of the wind had shifted and the ship could not get out of the natural harbor. They had to return to their first anchorage and await more favorable winds.

Khitrov drew the first known map of the outer Shumagin Islands, with a diagram indicating the various positions of their ship and boats during their stay in the area.

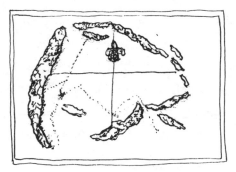

This map of the Shumagin Islands by Lt. Khitrov shows the anchorage of the St. Peter and Steller's and Khitrov's landing sites.

For weeks Steller had sought native Americans without success. He had discovered their still-warm fire pit, their storage cellar, and their trails—but not the people themselves. Now, when least expected, it was they who came to him. In his journal for September 4, 1741, Steller recorded the first European encounter with natives of the Pacific Northwest:

> We had scarcely dropped the anchor when . . . we saw two small boats paddling toward our vessel from shore. [The] men in their boats, while still paddling, began simultaneously to make an uninterrupted, long speech in a loud voice [which] we construed . . . as either a formula of prayer or incantation, or a ceremony of welcoming us as friends, since both customs are in use

in Kamchatka and the Kuril Islands . . . We . . . beckoned with our hands, that they might come nearer without being afraid of anything. They, in turn, however, pointed with the hand towards the land that we should come to them there, besides pointing with their fingers to the mouth and scooping up sea water with their hands as if to indicate that we could have food and water with them . . . One of them . . . took from the sticks lying behind him on the skin boat one which was like a billiard cue . . . of spruce wood and painted red, placed two falcon wings on it and tied them fast with whalebone, showed it to us, and then with a laugh threw it towards our vessel into the water . . . On our part we tied two Chinese tobacco pipes and some glass beads to a piece of board and tossed it to him.

Waxell wrote of the native people: "I could see that they were afraid and mistrustful, and I wanted to show them that we were not afraid and also to convince them that their fears of us were unfounded." The lieutenant chose a rather odd way to put them at their ease.

Although the sea was very rough, Bering gave Waxell permission to follow the natives to their island. With his improved position, Steller was now chosen to take part in this most important foray. In his journal he tells the story, leaving the part played by "our gentlemen" to be told in Waxell's own words.

After a short consultation the boat was let down, in which I, besides Lieutenant Waxell, the Koryak interpreter, and nine sailors and soldiers decided to pull ashore. We provided ourselves with lances, sabers, and guns but covered all with canvas so as not to arouse suspicion . . . The beach was very rocky, the tide rapidly rising; wind and waves were likewise so high that with the greatest difficulty we kept the boat from being dashed to pieces . . . As we saw that we ourselves had no hope of getting ashore, we let our interpreter and two other persons undress and go through the water to them . . . The islanders received the interpreter and the others in a very friendly way and led them by the arms, quite deferentially as if they were very great personages, to the place where they had been seated, presented them there with a piece of whale blubber, talked a bit with them, though nobody understood the other . . . [One of the Americans] got into his boat . . . and came paddling up to us.

Waxell described his own effort to make friends with the native leader:

He was evidently the eldest and I am sure also the most eminent of them all. I handed him a beaker of gin which he put to his lips, but spat the gin out again at once and turning to his fellows screeched most horribly. I had also wished to make him presents

of various trifles, such as needles, glass beads, a little iron kettle, tobacco-pipes and such like, but he would accept nothing from me and turned back again.

It is obvious that Waxell had lost their trust; their leader had become too suspicious to trade with such people.

In his account Waxell does not mention his second faux pas, but Steller continues:

Although I advised against [it], our gentlemen . . . gave the stranger a lighted pipe of tobacco, which he had accepted indeed, though paddling away quite disgusted. The smartest European

would have done just the same if he had been treated to fly mushroom or rotten fish soup and willow bark, which the Kamchadals, however, consider such delicacies.—As in the meantime the surf and wind were increasing more and more, our people were called back to the boat. The kind islanders, on the other hand, wanted their company still further and . . . kept them from the boat by force. Another party took hold of the painter with which our boat was made fast and intended . . . to haul the boat with its occupants ashore, where it would have been wrecked on the rocks. As in this confusion and danger there was no time to be lost and as the islanders could not be dissuaded from their purpose by sign language, shots were fired simultaneously over their heads at the rocks from three muskets loaded with balls . . . They all fell down on the ground as if hit by thunder, letting go of everything in their hands. Our men ran at once through the water and got safely into the boat . . . [The islanders] waved their hands to us to be off quickly as they did not want us any longer . . . [That night] our Americans . . . lighted a fire on shore and kept us pondering on what had happened.

It was a thoughtful ending to the day on which guns were introduced to Alaska.

Steller wrote the first European description of native Alaskans. Trained by months with the Itelmen, he relied on his excellent memory and his anthropologist's eye to write a detailed account when he returned to the ship. His hypothesis that the Americans had originally come from Kamchatka was based upon the similarities he noticed in the two peoples.

I counted nine islanders on the beach, mostly young or middle-aged people, they are of medium stature, strong and stocky, yet fairly well proportioned, and with very fleshy arms and legs. The hair of the head is glossy black and hangs straight down all around the head. The face is brownish, a little flat and concave. The nose is also flattened, though not particularly broad or large. The eyes are as black as coals, the lips prominent and turned up. In addition they have short necks, broad shoulders, and their body is plump though not big-bellied . . .

Finally, I observed also on all these Americans that they had a very scant beard, but most of them none at all, in which respect they again agree with the inhabitants of Kamchatka . . .

The American boats are about two fathoms long, two feet high, and two feet wide on the deck, pointed towards the nose but truncate and smooth in the rear . . . The frame is of sticks fastened together at both ends and spread apart by crosspieces inside. On the outside this frame is covered with skins, perhaps of seals, and colored a dark brown. With these skins the boat is [covered] flat above but sloping towards the keel on the sides . . .

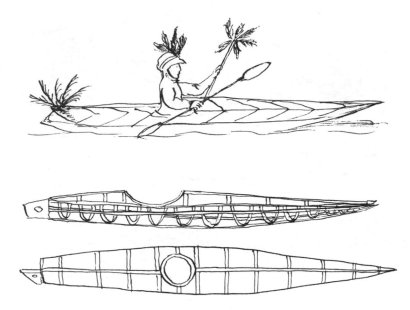

About [five feet] from the rear on top is a circular hole, around
the whole of which is sewn [a strip made of] whale guts having a
hollow hem with a leather string running through it, by means
of which it may be tightened or loosened like a purse. When the
American has sat down in his boat and stretched out his legs under the deck, he draws this hem together around his body and
fastens it with a bowknot in order to prevent any water from getting in . . . The American puts his right hand into the hole of the
boat and, holding the paddle in the other hand, carries it thus because of its lightness on to the land anywhere he wants to and
back from the land into the water. The paddle consists of a stick
a fathom long, at each end provided with a shovel, a hand wide.
With this he beats alternately to the right and to the left into the
water and thereby propels his boat with great adroitness even
among large waves.

Steller's theory that these Americans—the Unalaskan branch of
the Aleuts—came originally from Kamchatka is accepted today.

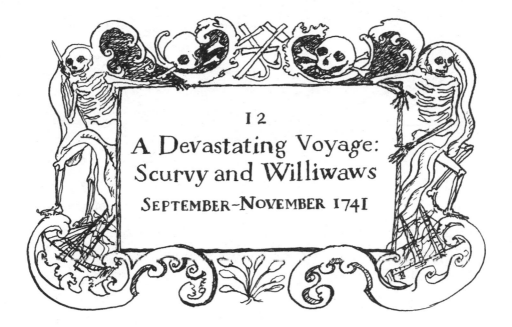

12
A Devastating Voyage: Scurvy and Williwaws
SEPTEMBER–NOVEMBER 1741

THE NEXT MORNING A SECOND GROUP OF AMERICANS paddled out to the ship. Their faces were pierced and decorated with pieces of bone; Steller compared the practice to European ear piercing. The Americans traded two of their visor-like hats adorned with small ivory figures for an iron kettle and some needles and thread. Noticing that the natives had no weapons, Waxell suggested that he capture several of them, but Bering would not hear of it. The Senate's orders were to give presents and establish friendly relations with any natives they might meet and not to antagonize them in any way.

That day the wind changed and the *St. Peter* was able to escape the confines of the harbor and continue the return voyage.

Steller wrote of the condition of his shipmates:

The unwholesome water lessened the number of healthy men from day to day, and very many were heard to complain of hitherto unwanted disorders . . . The Captain Commander, who from

scurvy and confinement had entirely lost the use of his limbs, was restored by me to such an extent simply by his partaking of the fresh spoonwort that within eight days he could get out of bed and on deck again and felt as well as at the beginning of the voyage.

Unfortunately, new men soon began to suffer from scurvy, and now there were no herbs to cure them. Two weeks later one of the grenadiers died. On October 27, the assistant navigator, Yushin, who was keeping the ship's second log with Hesselberg, wrote, "I have such pains in my feet and hands, owing to the scurvy, that I can with difficulty stand my watch. 32 on the sick list."

Throughout September and October the *St. Peter* was battered by storm after storm, barely escaping shipwreck as its crew attempted to chart the islands of what we now call the Aleutian chain on their return to Kamchatka. Winds drove them miles off course,

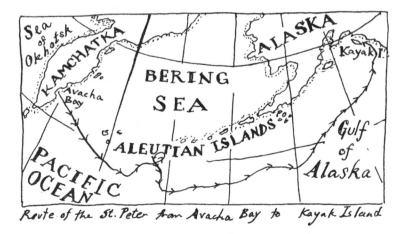

Route of the St. Peter from Avacha Bay to Kayak Island

back toward Alaska. The area they traversed is notorious for some of the most dramatic weather on earth. Within a few minutes a calm, sunny day might change into a black hailstorm with williwaws lashing the sails.

One can easily imagine the agony of the sick, longing for home
or for death, unable to sleep or even to rest as their ship was tossed
about on the waves. They knew the longitude and latitude of
Avacha Bay, but they could not chart their course by the stars during stormy, cloudy nights. As sailor after sailor died, the journey
seemed endless and without hope.

SEPTEMBER 27

We again had a very violent storm
from the southeast . . . Every now
and then we could hear the wind
rush as if out of a narrow passage,
with such terrible whistling, raging, and blustering that we were
every minute in danger of losing masts or rudder or else of seeing
the vessel itself damaged by the force of the waves, which
pounded it as when cannons are fired, so that we were expecting
every moment the last stroke and death. Even the old and experienced pilot, Andreas Hesselberg, could not recall among the experiences of his fifty years at sea having passed through a storm
which even resembled it.

Only three days later, an even more terrifying storm descended.

SEPTEMBER 30

About five o'clock in the morning, we encountered a storm from
the southwest of such redoubled violence as we never have experienced before or since; we could not imagine that it could be
greater or that we should be able to stand it out. Every moment
we expected the destruction of our vessel, and no one could lie
down, sit up, or stand. Nobody was able to remain at his post; we
were drifting under the might of God whither the angry heavens

willed to send us. Half of our crew lay sick and weak, the other half were of necessity able-bodied but quite crazed and maddened from the terrifying motion of the sea and ship. There was much praying, to be sure, but the curses piled up during ten years in Siberia prevented any response. Beyond the ship we could not see a fathom out into the ocean because we continuously lay buried among the cruel waves. Furthermore, we could neither cook nor have anything cold to eat except half-burnt biscuits, which were already beginning to run short. Under such conditions no one any longer possessed either courage or counsel . . . Let no one imagine that our situation is here represented as too dangerous, let him rather believe that the most eloquent pen would have found itself too weak to describe our misery.

Just as scurvy was taking its toll on the men, the wild sea and battering winds were tearing the ship asunder. Rigging snapped, sails ripped, and on October 1 the gun port bulwark was carried out to sea. The men could do no more than hammer boards over the gaping hole in the deck.

When we had scarcely more than four able-bodied men left on the vessel, I was tearfully begged to help and assist, which then, though with empty hands, I did to the utmost of my strength and means, although it was not my office and my services had always been scorned before the disaster.

As doctor, minister, and now volunteer crew member, Steller did all he could to encourage the men and save their ship, inspiring

others to do the same. The four healthy men were Steller, and probably those with whom he had shared fresh greens while anchored by
the Shumagin Islands a month before—Plenisner, Toma, and perhaps Betge. During the next month the weather, the health of the
captain and crew, and the condition of the ship itself all went from
bad to worse, as noted in Steller's journal entries from October 24
to 31.

> Misery and death suddenly got the upper hand on our ship to
> such an extent that not only did the sick die off, but those who
> according to their own assertion were well, on being relieved at
> their posts, dropped dead from exhaustion. The small allowance
> of water, the lack of biscuits and brandy, the cold, dampness,
> nakedness, vermin, fright, and terror were not the least impor-
> tant causes.

With so many ill, it became almost impossible to make changes
in the sails. But on the morning of November 4, a new hope appeared on the horizon.

> To our great astonishment it chanced that towards nine
> o'clock land was seen. It is impossible to describe how great and
> extraordinary was the joy of everybody at this sight. The half-
> dead crawled up to see it, and all thanked God heartily for this
> great mercy.

The next day, snow was falling on the deck outside while a
ship's council was being held at Bering's bedside. Before the council, Waxell and Khitrov had met privately and decided that the
ship should land immediately. At the ship's council they found that
Bering instead wished to sail on to Avacha Bay, rather than arrive at
random somewhere along the coast of Kamchatka. With a warm

bed and fresh food, he might have hoped to recover his health. Waxell then asked the opinion of Ovtsin, Bering's assistant. Loyal to Bering at this crucial juncture of the voyage, Ovtsin replied that he agreed with the Captain Commander: he preferred to sail on to Avacha Bay. In his journal Steller described the scene that followed. Waxell and Khitrov turned on Ovtsin, shouting, " 'Get out, hold your tongue, scoundrel, rascal!' and so he had to leave the council."

> At last . . . my turn came also; but warned by the example of Ovtsin I answered: "I have never been consulted in anything from the beginning, nor will my advice be taken if it does not agree with what is wanted; besides, the gentlemen themselves say that I am not a sailor; therefore I would rather not say anything."—I was next asked if I . . . would not at least add a written certificate regarding the sickness and the miserable condition of the crew.— This I thereupon undertook to do, in accord with my conscience.

The crew and petty officers were willing to go ashore only if the land was certainly Kamchatka. In response, Khitrov rashly declared that if it were not, he would let his head be cut off.

Steller recalled the scene as the ship sailed toward the shore, chaos prevailing until Ovtsin took command.

It was now already night but very light on account of the moon . . . The ship was tossed about like a ball and . . . it also snapped the anchor cable, so that we expected nothing short of being wrecked. The confusion became still greater by the constant breaking of the waves, the shouting and the wailing, so that no one any longer knew who should give or who should take orders . . .

One asked, "Is the water very salty?" as if death were sweeter in sweet water . . .

Ovtsin and the boatswain came forward [and] advised . . . to let the vessel drift. When we had thus passed inside the bar and the surf, these men, who alone had retained their reason, let the last anchor drop, because we now lay between the *burun* [heavy surf] and the shore as in a placid lake.

13
Kamchatka
or a
Barren Island?
NOVEMBER–DECEMBER 1741

THE NEXT DAY STELLER, PLENISNER, AND TOMA WERE THE first to row toward land with several of the sick men. They had not yet reached the shore when they were greeted by the strange sight of a crowd of animals swimming in their direction. At first they took them to be bears or wolverines. It was disconcerting to find that they were sea otters, animals much hunted in Kamchatka for their exquisitely soft pelts. If this was Kamchatka, why were the otters so fearless of men?

Freezing winds blew over the snow-covered landscape as Plenisner went off to hunt ptarmigan while Steller investigated the surrounding area. In the evening they returned to the sick men, finding Waxell, very weak and faint, with his son. As they attempted to warm themselves with tea, Steller remarked, "God knows whether this is Kamchatka!" To which Waxell replied, "What else can it be? We shall soon send for horses."

Waxell returned to the ship while Steller and his companions found a good campground near a stream. After their tent was blown

away by a gale, Steller showed the crew how to dig shallow versions of the Kamchadal underground dwellings, supporting the walls with driftwood and roofing them with sails. The men would not have been strong enough to dig through the earth had it been a solid frozen block, but fortunately the soil was sandy and the site was honeycombed with fox burrows. If the men broke through their walls, snug chambers could be formed—Steller, with his dark sense of humor, referred to them as "our 'grave.'"

On shipboard Steller had shown himself willing to work as hard as any crew member. The same was true on land.

> We all realized that rank, learning, and other distinctions would be of no advantage here in the future or suffice as a means of sustenance; therefore, before being driven to it by shame and necessity, we ourselves decided to work with what strength we had still left, so as not to be laughed at afterward or wait until we were ordered . . .

NOVEMBER 8

I had to encourage my sick and feeble Cossack . . . thus making the first step to our future companionship. "Be of good cheer," I said, "God will help. Even if this is not our country, we have still hope of getting there; you will not starve; if you cannot work and wait on me, I will do it for you; I know your upright nature and what you have done for me; all that I have belongs to you also; only ask and I will divide with you equally until God helps."—But he said: "Good enough; I will gladly serve Your Majesty, but you have brought me into this misery. Who compelled you to go with these people? Could you not have enjoyed the good times on the Bolshaya River?"—I laughed heartily at his frankness and said: "God be praised, we are both alive! If I have dragged you into this misery, you have in me, with God's help, a lifelong friend and benefactor. My intentions were good, Toma, so let yours be good also; moreover, you do not know what might have happened to you at home."

    . . . In the evening, as we were sitting around the camp fire after having eaten our meal, a blue fox came up and took away two ptarmigans right before our eyes. This was the first sample of the many tricks and thefts which those animals practiced on us later.

Steller frequently mentions the wily and infuriating blue foxes in his journal. From his first moments on land the boldness of the foxes furthered his suspicions that the ship had not reached Kamchatka—the foxes were fearless and showed no signs of having been hunted by the Itelmen.

    The foxes, which now turned up among us in countless numbers, became accustomed to the sight of men and, contrary

to habit and nature, ever tamer, more wicked, and so malicious
that they dragged apart all the baggage, ate the leather sacks,
scattered the provisions, stole and dragged away from one his
boots, from another his socks and trousers, gloves, coats, all of
which yet lay under the open sky and for lack of ablebodied men
could not be protected. They even dragged off iron and other im-
plements that were of no use to them. There was nothing they
did not sniff at and steal from . . . At the same time, they made
us laugh in our greatest misery by their crafty and comical monkey tricks . . .

This animal . . . far surpasses the common fox in impudence,
cunning, and roguishness . . . However well we might bury
something and weight it down with stones, they not only found
it but, like human beings, pushed the stones away with their
shoulders and, lying under them, helped each other [do this]
with all their might. If we cached something up in the air on a
post they undermined the post so that it had to fall down or one
of them climbed up it like a monkey or a cat and threw down the
object with incredible skill and cunning. They observed all that
we did and accompanied us on whatever project we undertook. If
an animal was cast up by the sea they devoured it even before one
of us could reach it, to our great detriment; and if they could not

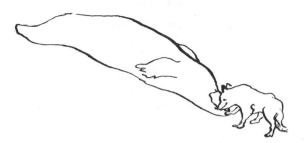

eat it all up at once they dragged it piecemeal to the mountains
[and] hid it from us under stones . . . While doing this others
stood guard and watched out for the arrival of any of the men.

Close to the shore lived huge creatures that reminded Steller of the South American manatees he had read about in St. Petersburg. Toma, who had traveled all over the Kamchatka Peninsula with Krasheninnikov, told Steller that this extraordinary animal was unknown to him.

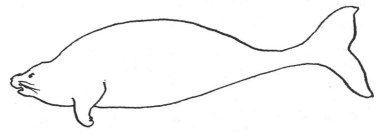

NOVEMBER 10

More sick [men] were brought ashore, among them also the Captain Commander . . . I . . . wondered at his composure and singular contentment. He asked what my idea was about this land.—I answered that it did not look to me like Kamchatka; the great number and tame assurance of the animals of itself clearly indicated that it must be sparsely inhabited or not at all . . . I mentioned at the same time the unknown sea animal, manati, which I had seen . . . To all this I got the reply: "The vessel can probably not be saved, may God at least spare our longboat."

As they became familiar with the land, the men gave names to different places—Wood Creek, where they often found logs washed ashore, Sea Otter Rock, Sea Lion Bay, Whale Creek, where they discovered a stranded animal, and the Impassable Rock, which

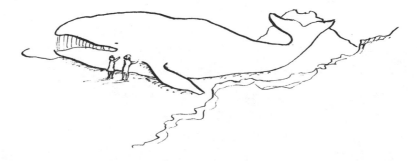

blocked their way along the coast. Those who were well enough to work divided themselves into three parties. The first waded through the ice-cold water to bring back provisions from the ship or rowed the men ashore in the longboat. The second dragged driftwood logs from Wood Creek to reinforce and roof the underground dwellings. The third, comprising a sick Russian cannoneer, who

was building a sled for hauling, and Steller, who was acting as doctor, minister, and cook, remained at the camp.

Steller noticed that the men now treasured objects once taken for granted "such as axes, knives, awls, needles, thread, shoe twine, shoes, shirts, socks, sticks, strings, and similar things which in former days many of us would not have stooped to pick up."

As Steller carefully nursed Bering during his last illness, a new bond of respect and affection formed between them.

NOVEMBER 13

While thus taking upon myself the office of cook I . . . visit[ed] the Captain Commander off and on and to assist him in various ways . . . It also became my duty to succor some of the weak and sick and to bring them warm soups, continuing this until they had recovered somewhat and were able to take care of themselves.

The men who were dying or recovering from scurvy were put into a dugout infirmary where Steller looked after them until they either were well enough to join one of the dwellings or were dead and buried.

In his narrative pieced together from survivors' accounts, the historian of the Second Kamchatka Expedition, Professor Gerhard Friedrich Müller, who knew Steller's character after spending seven weeks with him in Yeniseisk, described the naturalist's role on the island: "They could not lose heart, because they had Steller with them. Steller was a doctor who at the same time ministered to the spirit; he cheered everyone with his lively and agreeable company."

NOVEMBER 15

We had only a three months' supply of summer clothing and shoes, [and] much became torn every day because of the hard work . . . Since nobody would work for money, everyone had to act as shoemaker, tailor, glover, butcher, carpenter, cook, and footman as best he could, so that henceforth they would have been able to earn an ample living in all these trades.

After months of drinking brackish water, Steller wrote this appreciation:

All the water, that of the inland lakes as well as the streams, is, because of the stony bottom and the rapid motion, unusually cold, pure, and light, in other words, wholesome. Its good effect on our sick and emaciated bodies we all experienced with great profit and joy.

In Kamchatka, as an experiment, Steller had lived on native foods without bread and found he stayed as healthy as ever. He felt confident that with freshwater and a varied diet many of the men could regain their health. But at the same time he saw Bering's life ebbing away, and he could do no more than try to make him comfortable. Bering had recovered from scurvy but continued to suffer from several other ailments, especially a heart condition. He felt warm only when he was virtually buried up to his neck in sand, and he was plagued by fleas and lice, apparently even more than the other men.

For a time Waxell and Khitrov had stayed on the ship, thinking they would be more comfortable in a cabin than in a sandy underground dwelling. But scurvy is greatly aggravated by lack of movement, and by the time they decided to go ashore, they were much more ill than on the day they had arrived.

> Finally Waxell himself was also brought ashore. He was so badly ravaged by the scurvy that we abandoned all hope for his life, but nevertheless we did not fail to come to his help with both food and medicine . . . We were all the more anxious for his recovery, as . . . after his decease . . . the supreme command would fall to Khitrov . . . In spite of [Waxell's] urgent entreaty we could not take him into our hut, but we promised to assist so that a separate one could be built for him and a few other patients.

Now that Bering, Waxell, and Khitrov were bedridden and desperately ill, the crew turned to Steller for guidance. He fed them, nursed them, prayed with them, and established a fellow feeling among them, so that each man would assist the others and not merely look out for himself. He gathered salad greens that resembled nasturtiums, made ptarmigan soup, and turned to the Kamchadal way of cooking cormorants in wet clay. He hoped they would not be reduced to eating the scavenging foxes. Every skill he had, as doctor, minister, and cook, was required to save the expedition.

Steller appears to have regretted being unable to have Waxell in his hut, whether for lack of space or for some other reason, but his Christian charity did not extend to Khitrov.

NOVEMBER 15

All the sick were finally brought ashore . . .

Master Khitrov begged us fervently, for God's sake, to take him into our partnership and to assign him a corner because he could not possibly lie among the ordinary seamen who day as well as night reproached him for all kinds of past affairs, accused him of all kinds of mistreatment, and let out all kinds of threats. He said he could not stand it any longer, and he would consequently have to die under the open sky. But because our dwelling was already crammed full and no one was allowed to take action on anything without the foreknowledge of the others, we were all opposed because we were all offended by him, and we refused him all hope, because he was healthy and lazy, and he alone had plunged us into this misfortune.

From the moment Khitrov left Okhotsk, his poor judgment and worse luck had brought nothing but hardship to everyone. When he grounded the *Nadezhda* on the sandbar in the Okhotsk harbor, losing much of the ship's biscuit, he made it impossible for the expedition to overwinter in America. In the Shumagin Islands, when he failed to return to the vessel before the storm broke, they lost five days of excellent winds at a critical time and the yawl was damaged beyond repair. When he insisted that they had reached Kamchatka and would not listen to anyone else's opinion, once again he endangered the lives of everyone on board, especially the Captain Commander. And now here they were, probably on an island, with most of the men sick, their captain dying, and their ship, run aground on a rock in the harbor, ready to be washed away by the next violent storm, the men too weak to bring it ashore. The *St. Peter* was so battered that it was doubtful it could ever sail again.

From Steller's journal one recognizes Khitrov as a coward and a braggart; from Waxell's account he seems a boon companion. Certainly the common seamen, not knowing their future, blamed him as they lay next to their dead and dying comrades who were being eaten by foxes even before breathing their last breath.

After noting that they had found no trace of human habitation, Steller wrote of the anxious dread they all experienced at this time:

> We were in daily fear that our vessel . . . might be driven out to sea and that with it we should lose at one stroke all our provisions and our hope of deliverance.

Just when their situation was looking hopeless, they awoke after a storm to a wonderful change. During the night, the sea had tossed the *St. Peter* up onto the beach into a better position than

they could ever have dragged it. Previously the men had had to carry provisions ashore by wading out to the ship neck-deep in icy water; now they had all their supplies within easy reach, and while they found they could not make the *St. Peter* seaworthy again, at least they could use her as salvage for building a new vessel.

Vitus Bering died a few days later, as if released from life by knowing the fate of his ship.

After recording in his journal the deaths of five crew members, Steller went on to write of Bering, who died on December 8, 1741:

He would undoubtedly have remained alive if he had reached Kamchatka and had only had the benefit of a warm room and fresh food. As it was, he perished rather from hunger, cold, thirst, vermin, and grief than from any disease.

In his will Bering entrusted his two servants to Steller, as if to make amends for the times Steller asked for help on the Shumagin and Kayak islands and Bering had failed to respond.

14
Bering Island
DECEMBER 1741

~

MAY 1742

I T TOOK SOME TIME TO CONFIRM THAT THEY WERE ON AN
island, although Steller had suspected it from the first. Several
groups of crewmen attempted to follow the coastline. But sometimes the shore was blocked by cliffs, or the weather turned stormy
and they barely escaped from freezing to death in the snow. Everyone was finally convinced on April 7, 1742, however, when Khitrov
wrote in the ship's log, "Ivanov and his party returned and reported
that we were on an island."

They named the place Bering Island after their Captain Commander.

> After the death of our leader we had made so much progress
> that the entire command found itself in five underground
> dwellings secure against the severity of the winter . . . In front of
> each dwelling stood several barrels which served instead of a
> storehouse for keeping our supply of meat from the foxes.

Outside it was certainly cold enough to keep the meat fresh.

On shipboard each man was obedient to those superior to him in rank. On the island Steller led the way in establishing a more democratic arrangement by dividing the housekeeping among the ten men in his dwelling. While some of the men remained inside, cooking or helping in the kitchen, others went out hunting or fishing. Another party fetched water from the creek, while the rest collected driftwood for the fire. When a decision was to be made, all had an equal voice, independent of rank.

> Everyone knew at all times his duty and business without having to be reminded of it. This arrangement made all labor bearable and resulted in cheerfulness and good feeling among us and in our having greater abundance of better prepared food and drink than all the other households . . . Thus circumstanced, we celebrated Sundays and holidays, including holy Christmas.

Soon the men in the other four huts came to similar arrangements, following Steller's example.

Waxell's son Laurentz was not officially on the expedition. Rather than illegally giving him government provisions, Waxell had imposed upon himself the additional hardship of sharing his daily ration with his growing son. Waxell later wrote about the food on Bering Island:

Sea-otter flesh, which until March was our main means of sustenance, we ate at first with great repugnance, for it is very tough and consists mostly of sinews. It is almost like a piece of leather and has to be chewed, chewed and chewed again, before it becomes slightly softened and can be downed bit by bit. We could not bake bread of the little rye-flour that was alloted to each every month and we used it in the following ways: we stirred it up with warm water in a wooden bowl and let it stand for a couple of days till it had all fermented and turned sour, when we would put a few spoonfuls in a frying-pan and fry it in train-oil [whale oil rendered from a whale washed up on the beach]. This dish we found especially good, but we could not indulge too much as we had to eat twice a day of the little there was. This was especially very difficult for me, as I had my own son with me. He was a lad of twelve years and at that time a volunteer . . . The lad wanted to eat as much of our portion as I, and we made an agreement with each other, that the one who at midday had three spoonfuls of this bread-dish should in the evening have two.

While their first challenge was finding food, the second was gathering firewood on an island without a single tree. Waxell described their methods:

What contributed to our wretchedness was the fact that we were terribly short of fuel, so much so that every now and again we were forced to eat our various delicacies almost raw . . . When anyone found some driftwood he went straight back and informed the others in the hollow in which he lived, who joyfully set out with axes and ropes for the scene of the discovery. There, each chopped as large a pile of wood as he could take on his back and carried it back to his sand-hollow . . . We would go out searching for wood under the snow and whenever we saw anything rising above the flat surface, there we would dig, and sometimes we would find good pieces of wood. Such was the laborious method by which we had the whole time to find the little fuel of which we were able to get hold.

Another thing that incommoded us to the highest degree was the weather. Although at no time during the winter could we complain of great, penetrating cold, we did have violent hurricanes and stormy winds with thick snow. From the sea came thick mists and dampness that caused the sails covering our hollows in the sand to rot, until they were no longer able to withstand the violence of the storms, but were blown away on the first gust, leaving us lying under the open sky . . . The storms were so violent that on several occasions people getting out of their hollows to relieve nature were whirled away and would undoubtedly have been blown out to sea had they not thrown themselves on the ground and clung to a stone or anything else that they were able to seize. Even so, they had to remain lying there till the worst was over. I myself was once flung right across my pit when it was covered with a sail . . . I clung on as well as I could and shouted for help until the others came and, with great difficulty, brought me and themselves back into our pit.

The ship's hull was cracked and buried deep in the sand, its four anchors were lost in the harbor, and its rudder had been carried out to sea. The officers and crew agreed to dismantle the wreck of the *St. Peter* and build a smaller ship from its lumber. Then they would

refit it and sail back to Kamchatka. But all four of the ship's carpenters had died of scurvy. The situation looked desperate until they discovered that one of the crew members, Sava Starodubtsov, had worked for a few months as a laborer under Spangberg in the Okhotsk shipyard when the *St. Peter* was being built. Waxell wrote:

> He said that if I would give him the proportions of the new ship he would build it under my guidance and make her so solid that, with God's help, we should be able to put to sea in her without risk.

But how could they spare men for carpentry when everyone was needed for hunting? The sea mammals no longer used the beach near the campsite as a resting place; they had been frightened away. For the hunters, getting food involved trekking many miles across the island, killing sea otters or sea lions with clubs, and returning with the meat on their backs. At this point, Steller devised a method of hunting the huge, hitherto-unapproachable sea cows that fed in the waters just offshore. Their dense, two-layered skin was almost impossible to penetrate, but with harpoons and bayonets in the longboat, and thirty sailors with ropes on the beach, the crew succeeded in bring-

ing a sea cow to shore. The meat was delicious and kept well. One animal could feed the crew for a week. Fortified by their new diet, on April 9, 1742, they were ready to begin construction of the ship.

> Everything was taken out of the vessel, and the materials were brought together in one place on the beach; grindstones were dressed and placed in troughs, tools were cleaned of rust and sharpened, a smithy erected, crowbars, iron wedges, and large hammers forged, wood gathered, and charcoal made.

The officers were always first at the construction site, setting a good example for the crew. But Steller's talents were needed elsewhere.

May 5

> The pleasant spring weather brought us still other advantages, besides the mild air, for, after the snow had thawed, we discovered here and there on the beach so much wood that we felt quite encouraged with regard to the charcoal necessary for the work in the smithy. We furthermore obtained many edible and palatable herbs and roots, which, besides being a change, served as medicine for our emaciated bodies.

After Shumagin Island, Waxell had come to respect Steller's knowledge of natural history and medicine, while Steller learned to appreciate Waxell's cheerful personality. In his account of the expedition, Waxell later wrote:

As soon as the snow was gone, and green shoots came out of the ground, we collected and used quantities of herbs and plants. In this Adjunct Steller gave excellent assistance, for he was a good botanist. He collected and showed us many green herbs, some for drinking, some for eating, and by taking them we found our health noticeably improved . . . None of us became well or recovered his strength completely before we began eating something green, whether plant or root.

On Bering Island, Steller used some of the following plants against scurvy:

1. Kamchatkan sweet grass
2. Bulbs of the sarana lily, much more plentiful and larger than in Kamchatka
3. The roots of a kind of angelica
4. The leaves of the sea lungwort
5. The young shoots of the purple fireweed
6. The roots of the bistort
7. The leaves of the upland cranberry, from which an infusion was made to substitute for black tea
8. True wintergreens, or shinleafs, and, as a second choice speedwells, to substitute for green tea
9. Scurvy grass, beccabunga, and bitter cress

When the May rains thawed the frozen ground and the floors of the underground dwellings became flooded, Steller remembered the Kamchadal response to spring. The men built summer homes aboveground and abandoned their underground huts.

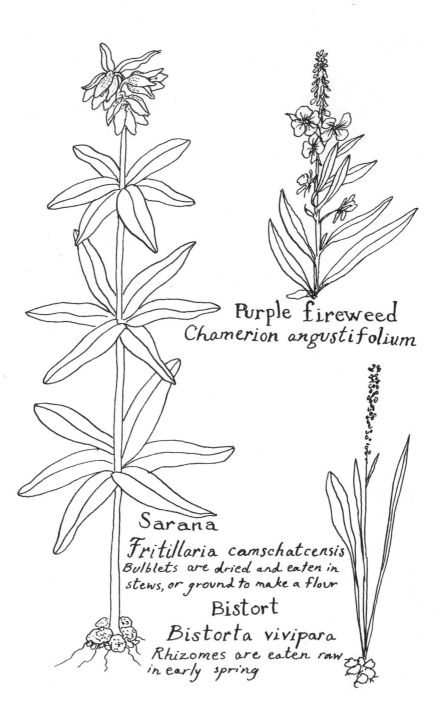

Purple fireweed
Chamerion angustifolium

Sarana
Fritillaria camschatcensis
Bulblets are dried and eaten in
stews, or ground to make a flour

Bistort
Bistorta vivipara
Rhizomes are eaten raw
in early spring

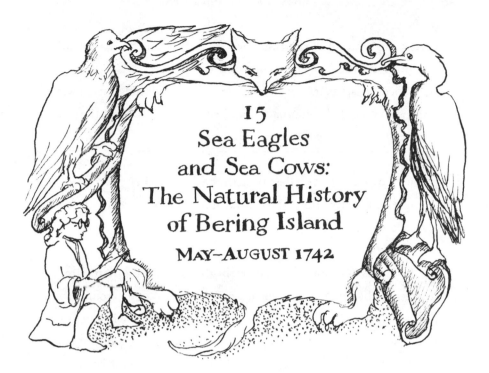

15
Sea Eagles and Sea Cows: The Natural History of Bering Island
MAY–AUGUST 1742

NOW, WITH EVERYONE'S HEALTH AND SPIRITS RESTORED and work on the ship progressing well, Steller was free to carry out his duties as mineralogist, examining the rocks and soil for precious metals. He could also explore the island in greater depth as a naturalist. For the next month, while the new ship was being constructed, he and Toma walked all around the island, observing the natural world. They lived entirely on food they hunted or found—flightless cormorants, birds' eggs, mollusks, sarana bulbs, and other plants. The naturalist came to know the island and its inhabitants intimately, beginning with the foxes raising their families.

In June they give birth to their young, nine to ten cubs, in caves and crevasses. They specially like to have their lairs up in the mountains . . . Their young ones they love so deeply that they

betray the location of their burrows by barking at human beings
like dogs in order to keep them from their young . . . As soon as
they notice that their burrow has been discovered they carry away
their young in their mouths . . . and endeavor to conceal them at
a more secluded place.

Steller climbed steep coastal cliffs and braved the wrath of outraged eagles to study their nesting habits. The bird was later named
Steller's sea eagle.

It makes its nest of brush on high cliffs. These nests are a
fathom in diameter and a foot high. It lays two eggs around the
beginning of June. The eaglets are totally white without any
spots. When I was inspecting the nest on Bering Island, the two
parents attacked me so forcefully I could barely fend them off
with a stick. Although I had not done the chick any harm, the
adult birds nevertheless deserted the nest and built another one
on a cliff where it was impossible for anyone to get to.

Only a strong man in good health could have withstood the attack of two sea eagles with their slicing beaks and nine-foot
wingspans.

Steller was the only scientist ever to describe, dissect, and eat the flightless spectacled cormorant. "From the ring around the eyes, and the clown-like twistings of the neck and head, it appears quite a ludicrous bird." It was as large as a goose, so that "the flesh of one would easily satisfy three hungry men." He cooked it in the way that he had prepared other species of cormorant  with the Kamchadals, wrapping the entire bird, feathers and all, in clay and cooking it in a fire pit—as Gypsies cook a hedgehog. When done, feathers and skin peeled off with the clay to expose the tender meat within.

Steller described many animals during his travels, but the most extraordinary was the sea cow, or northern manatee, later named in his honor. He was the only scientist ever to live in the company of these endearing sea mammals, more closely related to elephants than to whales. Indeed, no other scientist ever even saw one. Their flesh tasted like veal, and their fat was like the most delicate butter. Naturally, they became the favorite food of those who soon followed to hunt sea otters on Bering Island. Steller's sea cows became extinct only thirty years after he described them. The spectacled cormorant met the same fate some years later.

While living in his cramped underground hut and camping near rocky inlets around the island, Steller wrote his most celebrated work, *De Bestiis Marinis* (*The Beasts of the Sea*). The book is a study of the sea mammals on Bering Island—their anatomy, habits, temperament, and family life. Steller dissected and prepared speci-

mens of all the island's sea mammals, rewarding the sailors with precious tobacco for their help in dissecting the twenty-five-foot-long sea cow. His minute descriptions of their internal organs were made under the most difficult conditions, with foxes always in attendance, either trying to eat his specimen or mischievously running off with Steller's pen, paper, or ink.

Steller made the most of his exceptional situation, observing the social life of mammals never before described, at close range and for months on end. When his study of the sea otter was translated from Latin into English 150 years later, scientists who were trying to bring the animal back from the verge of extinction found there was next to nothing they could add to it.

Steller and Toma built makeshift huts from driftwood to shield themselves from the elements as they traveled around the island. They may also have used the huts as blinds so that their presence would not interfere with the animals' natural behavior.

SEA COW

Every day for ten months during our ill-fated adventure I had a chance to watch from the door of my hut the behavior and habits of these creatures and I will therefore briefly relate what I actually observed.

These animals love shallow and sandy places along the seashore, but they spend their time more particularly about the mouths of the gullies and brooks, the rushing fresh water of which always attracts them in herds . . .

They masticate differently from all other animals; not with teeth, which they lack altogether, but with two strong white bones, or solid tooth masses . . . corresponding . . . so perfectly that the seaweed is ground and mashed between them as . . . between millstones . . . These gluttonous animals eat incessantly . . . All they do while feeding is to lift the nostrils every four or five minutes out of the water, blowing out air and a little water with a noise like that of a horse snorting. While browsing they move slowly forward, one foot after the other, and in this manner half swim, half walk like cattle or sheep grazing. Half the body is always out of the water. Gulls are in the habit of sitting on the backs of the feeding animals feasting on the vermin infesting the skin, as crows are wont to do on the lice of hogs and sheep . . . The animal has no hair . . . It has bristles rather, or hollow quills, and these are found only around the mouth and under the feet . . . The feet are entirely without claws . . . so that the animal moves upon a skin that is rough with bristles.

Steller estimated that a full-grown adult weighed over twenty tons. He probably arrived at this figure by cutting up the animal and measuring the parts; he gives the dimensions of the different organs in his text.

When the tide came in, they came up so close to shore that I . . . sometimes even stroked their backs with my hand . . . [The animal] is covered with a thick hide, more like unto the bark of an ancient oak than unto the skin of an animal . . . black, mangy, wrinkled, rough, hard, and tough . . . They keep the young and the half-grown . . . in the middle of the herd. Most commonly whole families live together in one community, the male with one grown female and their tender little offspring.

Sea Bear or Fur Seal

For many years hunters had wondered where the sea bear, also known as the fur seal, went in the spring. Steller had studied the migration of salmon and birds on Kamchatka. He began his description of the fur seal by explaining why animals migrate.

> Birds and fishes migrate to lay their eggs . . . and because their strength is reduced or their feathers shed, and hence they are unable to flee from their foes until these can grow once more, solitary places are chosen by birds and quiet lakes by fishes . . . Accordingly, for a similar reason, these northern places are chosen by the sea bears . . . that the mothers may bear their young there upon the land and after parturition recruit their strength; further, that the young may there be brought up and nourished and may grow strong enough in three months to follow their parents home in the autumn . . .

> The pups are born with their eyes open, and their eyes are as large as those of a calf . . . In their first days [they] play together like children . . . and practice fighting until one throws the other

to the ground. When the father sees this he rises up with a growl and hastens to separate the combatants, kisses the victor, licks him with his tongue, tries with his mouth to throw him upon the ground, and makes vigorous demonstrations of his love for the youngster, who struggles bravely against it. In short, he rejoices that he has a son worthy of himself. But [the father is] less fond of the lazy and ease-loving pups. Hence some of the young are always near the father, others near the mother. The males are polygamous; one often has eight, fifteen, or even fifty wives. He guards them with anxious jealousy, and goes into a rage if another male comes ever so little too near . . .

These animals have three different kinds of speech. To pass away the time while they lie upon the land they cry out, and their voice is not at all different from the lowing of cows when deprived of their calves. In battle they roar and growl like a bear, and if they get the victory they utter a very sharp and often repeated note like our common crickets. But when wounded and overcome by their enemies they groan terribly or hiss like a cat or sea otter . . .

If I were required to state how many I saw on Bering Island I should truthfully say that I could not guess—they were countless, they covered the whole shore.

Sea Lion

Steller watched the ferocious, belligerent sea lions guarding their section of the beach and protecting their harems from competitors.

I lived a season in the midst of a herd of [sea lions, or
sivutch], and for six whole days on a spot above them, where
from my hut I watched their habits carefully . . . These beasts are
indeed terrible to look upon when alive, and they far surpass the
sea bear in strength and size as well as in endurance . . . They also
give to the eyes and mind the impression of a lion . . . If, when
they are sound asleep, a man comes up near and wakes them . . .
by a loud noise, they take to flight at once, panting like a fur-
nace, and with their limbs shaking so with fear that they can not
control them. But if one of them is cornered and all chance for
flight is shut off he turns against his enemy with a great roar,
shakes his head in wrath, rages, cries out, and puts even the
bravest man to flight. The first time that I tried this experiment
was almost the last of me. On this account this animal is never

hunted at sea by Kamchatkan tribes, because he overturns the
boat of the hunters and slays them most savagely . . .

The males [fight] jealously for their wives and for the best
places . . . One male has two, three, or four females. The pups are
born on land about the beginning of June . . .

[The sea lions] prey upon fish and seal especially, and also
upon otter and other sea animals.

At eventide the mothers with the young go out into the sea
and swim quietly near the shore. When the pups get tired of
swimming they are wont to perch upon the backs of their mothers and rest. But the mother rolls over like a wheel and shakes the
lazy pups off, and accustoms them to swimming . . .

They low like cows and the young bleat like sheep, and while I was among them it seemed to me as if I were playing the shepherd mingling with herds of cattle. [These beasts come to Bering Island] in June, July, and August . . . for quiet, for parturition, for rearing and teaching the pups, and for copulation . . . They are found in the Kuril Islands . . . Captain Spangberg on his chart has named a certain island from the number of these animals that he found upon it, and from a cliff overhanging their city, the "Palace of Sivutch."

SEA OTTER

Steller observed the Spartan behavior of sea lion mothers and the affectionate tenderness of mother sea otters.

As to the beauty of the animal, and particularly of its skin, this sea otter . . . surpasses all other inhabitants of the vast ocean . . . in point of beauty and softness of its fur.

As to its habits, it loves to live both in the water and on the land; but for the sake of sweet peace the otter inhabits in great droves, by preference, the great islands of the ocean. For getting food, it seeks, when the tide is out, the shallow, rocky reefs overgrown with seaweed, and there devours crustaceans, mussels, clams, snails, limpets, polyps, cuttlefish . . .

In the winter they lie some upon the ice, some upon the shore. In summer they go up the rivers and penetrate even to the lakes, where they greatly enjoy the fresh water. On warm days they seek the valleys and shady recesses of the mountains and frolic there like monkeys.

The females always give birth to their young on land.
Whether in the sea or on land, they carry their cubs in their
mouths; but when they sleep at sea they fold their young in their
arms just as mothers do their babes. They throw the young ones
into the water to teach them to swim, and when tired out they
bring them to shore again and kiss them just like human beings.
They toss the young out into the sea and with their paws catch
them when tossed, like a ball; and with them they engage in all
the delightful and gentle games that a fond mother can play with
her children . . .

They are very much afraid of sea lions and sea bears, and they
do not like the company of seals . . . The cry of the sea otter is
very like the cry of an infant. They doubtlessly live many years.
They never breed strife among themselves, but always live on the
best of terms with one another.

Lieutenant Khitrov drew this
map of the Commander Islands,
and, to the west, the Kamchatka
coastline. In the insert he drew
the Sea cow (above), and
Fur seal and Sea lion
(below) as he saw them on
Bering Island.

16
A Safe Return
to
Kamchatka
AUGUST 1742-JULY 1744

THROUGHOUT THE LONG WINTER, THE RETURN VOYAGE remained foremost in the minds of Steller and his companions. Present concerns always had to be balanced against future prospects. The cooks were careful not to encroach on the stores of flour reserved for the voyage home when making the fermented pancakes that supplemented the main food source of animals from the island. Steller wrote in his journal:

> It came to pass, as a result of [the work of] many hands, redoubled courage, and the constant efforts and friendly encouragement of Lieutenant Waxell, that in the month of July the vessel, 36 feet long at the keel and 42 feet from stem to stern, stood ready on the stocks as far as the hull was concerned. The remaining time until August 13 was consumed in making rigging . . . and finally also in building ways for launching the vessel . . . In the meantime some . . . were occupied in erecting an oven and in baking biscuits for the voyage; some overhauled the casks which

had to be bound for the voyage with iron hoops and ropes; some examined the bottom of the bay [for anchors]; and altogether there was no one who wanted to be idle, because everyone was exceedingly anxious for deliverance from this desert island.

The new *St. Peter* was considerably smaller than the original ship. Space was at a premium, even though thirty-two of the original seventy-eight men had died. Each sailor was restricted in his baggage. Most of the men used their space for the precious sea otter pelts skinned from the animals they had eaten. These would bring a high price, twenty rubles, in Kamchatka, and five times that at the market in Kyakhta on the Chinese border. Many members of the crew gave pelts to Steller in gratitude for his care when they were ill. Steller packed his manuscripts, seeds, and two of the sea cow chewing plates—what he had described as their "solid tooth masses"—but with the greatest reluctance and regret left behind the stuffed specimens—sea cow, fur seal, sea otter, and sea lion—that he had so carefully prepared.

Acting as ship's minister, Steller gathered the men for the christening of the new *St. Peter*.

August 13

All left their huts with much inner emotion and went on board the vessel, which was going either to bring us back to our country or to decide our fate in some manner or another . . .

At our departure we placed a wooden cross [on Bering's grave] which, according to the custom of the Russians in Siberia, is likewise the sign of a new country which has been subjected to the Russian Empire . . .

AUGUST 14

In the morning . . . the support of the Almighty was invoked in a special prayer for a good voyage, whereupon the anchors were weighed . . .

This afternoon we spent in high spirits since in bright and pleasant weather we passed by the island on which we knew all the mountains and valleys, whose paths we had climbed so many times with great effort to scout for our food and for other reasons and on which we had bestowed names from various circumstances and events. Thereby God's grace and mercy became manifested to all, the more brightly considering how miserably we had arrived there on November 6, had miraculously nourished ourselves on this barren island, and with amazing labor had become ever more healthy, hardened, and strengthened; and the more we gazed at the island on our farewell, the clearer appeared to us, as in a mirror, God's wonderful and loving guidance . . .

Early on Tuesday, the 17th, we suddenly caught sight of the mainland of Kamchatka . . . However, as under the lee of Kamchatka we had either complete calm or head winds the whole time, we spent nine days more in tacking, until at last, on the 26th of August, in the night, we arrived at the entrance of the bay [of Avacha] . . . and on the 27th, in the evening, in the long desired harbor itself.

Great as was the joy of everybody over our deliverance and safe arrival, nevertheless the news which we received from a Kamchadal . . . caused a much greater excitement. We had been regarded by everybody as dead or lost; the property which we had left behind had fallen into the hands of strangers and had mostly been carried away . . . However, we were all by this time so much used to misery and sorrow that . . . we . . . regarded the present circumstances as in a dream.

In Petropavlovsk, Steller learned what had become of their sister ship, the *St. Paul*. After sailing his ship to America and reaching Alaska about the time of Bering's arrival on Kayak Island, Captain Chirikov found he had only forty-five barrels of water remaining. He chose what appeared to be a safe landing place (which some scholars think was Takanis Bay, while others think it was Surge Bay) on Yakobi Island, south of Glacier Bay, and sent ten men with their fleet master ashore in the longboat to get water. The boat disappeared behind a headland. Although Chirikov saw fires burning on the beach at night, his signals went unanswered. After five days of waiting for a response, Chirikov sent his only remaining boat toward shore with a carpenter and tools in case the longboat was damaged. But that boat also disappeared. The next day, while they were expecting a signal, two boats came toward the ship from the mainland. The ship's crew rejoiced and set to work preparing to sail as soon as the boats reached them. But everyone's hopes were dashed when the boats came closer and they saw that they were kayaks paddled by native Americans. The boatmen waved to them and shouted words that sounded like "Agai! Agai!" but, refusing to come closer to the ship, they soon paddled back to shore.

With the water supply running low, and without boats in which to go ashore, Chirikov had no choice but to begin rationing water and to return to Kamchatka as swiftly as possible.

He assumed that his boatmen had been killed by native Americans, but scholars now believe that they never reached land. The boats were probably capsized by the deadly riptides at the mouth of either Takanis or Surge Bay. The Americans, who would have been Tlingit people, may have wanted to show them the remains of the boats that had washed ashore. What the Tlingit boatmen were saying is uncertain to this day.

On the return voyage, near Adak Island, the Russians were able to trade knives for water with some Aleuts who paddled out to their ship. The *St. Paul* arrived in Avacha Bay on October 9, 1741, while the *St. Peter* was still battling storms along the Aleutian chain. Of the seventy men on board the *St. Paul*, twenty-one succumbed to scurvy before reaching Kamchatka, the last being Professor de la Croyère, who died within sight of land. Everyone was ill by the time the vessel reached harbor.

The American part of the expedition was over, but it would be some months before word of the ships' return reached St. Petersburg and new instructions for Steller were issued by Professor Gmelin at the Academy of Sciences. Steller and Toma had had enough of ships. On August 27, 1742, they began a week's trek across the peninsula to Bolsheretsk. There Gorlanov presented Steller with a letter and a parcel from Brigitta Helena with the news that Empress Elizabeth had taken the throne. Before receiving his assignment, Steller had much work to do.

He edited his journal and arranged his collections of plants and animals. In an effort to improve education on the peninsula, he opened a school in Bolsheretsk for natives and Russians, hiring a schoolmaster with his own funds.

Steller spent the next year traveling through Kamchatka and considering new places to investigate. In Siberia there was a lively trade in fossil ivory from mammoth teeth and tusks. Steller had seen mammoth bones in Peter the Great's cabinet of curiosities. Recent finds near the mouth of the river Kolyma inspired him to write, "My soul is fired by the mammoth skeletons and the inadequate accounts of them."

In May 1743, he arranged to explore the more northern Kuril Islands. As he waited on the beach for his native boatmen, he discovered a large mollusk, now called the gumboot chiton. Its scientific name, *Cryptochiton stelleri*, stands as a tribute to Steller. He also found a starry flounder that he measured and described in Latin. Forty-five years later Pallas devised the witty name *Pleuronectes stellatus*.

He wintered in the far north with the Olyutor Koriaks, a tribe notorious for killing travelers and tax collectors. Even the Cossacks had been unable to subdue them. The tribe must have recognized Steller's sincere interest and genuine respect for them; he lived peaceably among them for several months. In the spring they allowed him to watch their shamans lead the whale hunting ceremony and then the whale hunt itself.

If you ask them the meaning of this ceremony, they only answer that their forefathers have done likewise and fared well and prospered by it.

As Steller traveled south by dogsled, he noticed that the sea was still frozen all the way to Karaga Island, not more than fifteen nautical miles offshore, where no naturalist had ever been. Impulsively, he decided to cross the ice and satisfy his curiosity. But the sheet of ice broke up under his weight halfway across. Steller lost his dogs and sled and nearly drowned in the frigid waters. He managed to return to the mainland only by strapping on his snowshoes and jumping from ice floe to ice floe, a technique he had observed among the hunters of sea otters off the Kuril Islands.

Steller probably refitted in Nizhnekamchatsk before traveling over the uninhabited Kamchatkan mountains and Cape Kronotski, collecting seeds and dormant plants as usual along the way. He found a stand of Kamchatka firs, endemic to the area near the mouth of the Semyatchik River. Steller rejoined his guide and

translator, Gorlanov, and his artist, Berckhan, in Bolsheretsk in the spring of 1744. He was full of ideas for further exploration and discovery but instead got embroiled in native unrest.

The Itelmen had rebelled against the Cossacks after the hardships imposed by the First Kamchatka Expedition, and again when Khitrov forced them to leave their families and travel long distances carrying his ship's supplies. Brutal retaliation by the Cossacks, along with the diseases introduced by them, had reduced the native population to about one-thirtieth of its original size. In 1744, Steller was struck by the many deserted villages along the banks of the rivers. He trusted and admired the Itelmen and felt that if they were well treated they would become loyal Russian citizens. He had learned much from them already. They had taught him how to construct underground winter dwellings and, more important, to identify the antiscorbutic plants that had saved the crew of the *St. Peter*. Soon he had the opportunity to show his gratitude and trust.

Steller described the event that would change his life:

> An overreaching and misunderstood order . . . caused a great deal of uneasiness in Kamchatka . . . Seventeen natives were needlessly dragged by four Cossacks 467 miles to Bolsheretsk Ostrog as rebels, for the purpose of being examined by me. They

told of having been informed by the Cossacks that an order had been issued to exterminate gradually the entire Itelmen nation. However, they could not believe this possible, and as baptized Christians, conscious of their loyalty and innocence, they had allowed themselves to be brought in, although as *tayons* [native chiefs] they could not have been forced by four Cossacks. If it was true that their extermination had been decided upon and ordered, they would rather yield themselves up to be slaughtered than lay themselves open to the suspicion of disobedience: "May God's and Her Imperial Majesty's will and order be done."

Steller recognized the men's innocence and allowed them to return to their villages. Then he sent a scathing letter to the Senate in St. Petersburg, accusing Vasily Khmetevski, the highest-ranking naval officer in Bolsheretsk, of disobeying the imperial orders not to provoke or ill-treat the natives of Kamchatka. Khmetevski, for his part, also wrote to the Senate and to the governor of Irkutsk, accusing Steller of being a traitor and of acquitting some "Kamchadal arch conspirators." Reports took so long to reach St. Petersburg, and Siberia was such an immense place in which to find someone, that more than a year passed before the charges made against Steller caught up with him.

17
Steller on Trial
AUGUST 1744
—
NOVEMBER 1746

IN AUGUST 1744, STELLER, BERCKHAN, AND GORLANOV SET sail from Bolsheretsk with sixteen packing cases of manuscripts and specimens. Danilov, who had acted as Steller's guide and translator throughout Siberia, joined their party in Okhotsk, and together they traveled over the Yablonoi Mountains to Yakutsk, then south on the Lena River to Irkutsk in the spring of 1745. There Steller was finally arrested on Khmetevski's charges of inciting Itelmen to rebel. Lorenz Lange, the scholarly vice governor of the Irkutsk region, heard Steller's case and released him at once. However, Lange neglected to send his report to St. Petersburg until the end of January, after the prolonged Christmas celebrations. Steller and his friends continued across Siberia, assuming the Senate had been informed of his innocence and that he would have no further trouble.

Danilov, Gorlanov, and Berckhan went on to Kazan with some of the cases of dried specimens, while Steller spent the spring and summer with Grigory Demidov, a wealthy landowner in Solikamsk. Demidov used the fortune his family had amassed from manufacturing cannons for Peter the Great and from mining gold, copper, and silver to surround himself with beautiful gardens and greenhouses, where he could raise plants otherwise too fragile for

the Siberian climate. He enjoyed the company of men of science. Three years earlier, Professor Johann Georg Gmelin had spent three weeks on the estate on his way back to St. Petersburg.

Steller's collection of dormant living plants had been safe in the frost. When they began to leaf out in the spring, however, they became more likely to suffer damage on the road. Steller planted them and some of his large collection of seeds in the Demidov greenhouses to fortify them for the last stage of the journey to St. Petersburg. He planned to transport them in the autumn, when they had

produced new seed or were dormant again. The raspberry from Kayak Island was among them.

Demidov, an amateur botanist, was delighted to explore the

flora of the Ural Mountains with so intelligent and knowledgeable a guest, a naturalist who had studied the plants of Siberia, even in the remote Barguzin Mountains. Now they could spend the spring and summer together in the field. Steller was eager to collect blooming specimens of plants he had found only in seed when he traveled that way in the summer at the beginning of his journey, almost eight years earlier.

The Senate in St. Petersburg, which had agents throughout Siberia, heard that Steller had arrived and departed from various towns. Having received Khmetevski's accusations but not Lange's report of Steller's innocence, the Senate suspected Steller of trying to evade the law. It sent a courier, Zakhar Lupandin, with orders to find and arrest Steller and immediately bring him to trial in Irkutsk. On August 16, 1746, Lupandin caught up with Steller, who had just returned to the Demidov estate, laden with plants from a long excursion into the Ural Mountains. Two years had passed since Steller's trial in Irkutsk—years, moreover, of travels and adventures. He could not imagine what he had done to displease the government. The courier had no explanation, only instructions. Orders were orders: Lupandin was authorized to allow Steller a single day to arrange his affairs, his life's work.

Steller wrote a distracted letter, a strange mixture of deference, obedience, and distress, to the director of the Academy of Sciences. His handwriting, usually so elegant, straight, and regular, became erratic and shaky. He had the highest respect for the Academy, and the letter reflects his desperation.

This sudden separation of my person from my work and my collections . . . may result in greatly lessening, if not entirely wrecking, my best endeavors, the honor of the Academy and the interests of Science . . . My conduct and actions are familiar to all who know me . . . With considerable peril to life and limb I have

at all times endeavored to advance the honor and lofty interests of
Your Imperial Majestic Academy of Sciences . . .

If [my collections] are found not to be in such shape as I
could wish, those who understand will not put the blame on me
but on the hurried transportation and jolting of the wagon and
on the importunate customs inspectors . . .

In Solikamsk my herbs and minerals collected in Perm remain without classification; the journal, however, I carry with
me. It has been impossible to get everything ready for transportation in one day. If they be sent away without me, the result will
be *pragan* [topsy-turvy] and all my labor lost; [not] only that,
[but] I will lose my reputation with those who have no knowledge of my exertions and precipitate departure.

He pictured his life's work scattered to the four winds, labels
and notebooks separated from the specimens they described or lost
entirely. Lacking the context of his observations and conclusions,
his collections, he feared, would be reduced to a meaningless accumulation of plants and animals. No wonder he was in despair.

For six weeks, Steller traveled under arrest with his courier before they were met in the town of Tara by another courier bearing
orders for Steller's release. The Senate, having finally received the
statement of Steller's innocence from Lange, had sent this second
courier to give Steller his freedom.

Steller left the next day for Tobolsk, where he celebrated his lib-
erty. There Archbishop Antonii Narozhnitski, once a student of
Steller's old friend Archbishop Feofan, entertained him splendidly.

In many Siberian towns the water was not safe and fevers spread rapidly among the population. A few years before, Gmelin described a fever he had in Tara. It "was over in eight days . . . and had no other bad results than that all my hair on the head fell out, though it came back gradually."

Now, in Tobolsk, Steller caught a dangerous fever but chose to ignore it rather than delay his return to St. Petersburg. He had survived when so many had died on Bering Island; he had lived through fevers in Halle and Tomsk; he was only thirty-seven years old—and was he not a *Sonntagskind*? Surely his good fortune would protect him. The Archbishop tried to reason with him, but to no avail. Was Steller too feverish to remember that Elias had nursed him in Halle and Danilov and Decker in Tomsk, not allowing him to travel until he was thoroughly recovered?

His driver harnessed the three horses, bundled Steller into the covered troika, and set off along the snowy track at a quick pace. They easily crossed the frozen Irtysh and Ob rivers.

Steller was critically ill by the time he reached Tyumen on November 12, 1746. Two German doctors who had sailed on the *St. Paul* happened to be in the town. They stayed by Steller's side until his death that evening, comforting him in his native tongue but unable to save him.

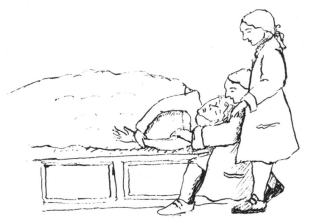

A Protestant could not be buried in the consecrated ground of Tyumen's Russian Orthodox cemetery. A visiting Lutheran minister wrapped Steller's body in his own red mantle and performed the burial service on a bluff overlooking the river Tura. That night grave robbers came, unearthed the corpse, and, stealing the precious religious garment, left the body as prey to scavenging dogs and wolves. Steller's friends, however, were able to restore his body to the ground, this time placing a boulder over the grave as its only marker.

WHEN TRAVELING THROUGH SIBERIA ON THE ACADEMY EXPEDItion of 1768–74, the naturalist Peter Simon Pallas made a pilgrimage to Tyumen in December 1770. He climbed to the top of the bluff and stood beside the boulder marking Steller's grave. Looking down upon the river where it flowed around the foot of the bluff, he recognized the remains of mammoths lying on the gravel by the riverside. He knew that in a century or two, Steller's bones, released from the crumbling cliff face, would rest with the ancient bones on the far side of the river Tura.

fragile rockbrake
*Cryptogramma
stelleri*

Steller's wormwood
Artemisia stelleriana

speedwell
Veronica stelleri

Alaska bellheather
Harrimanella stelleriana

AFTERWORD

SUCH WAS THE SECRECY ENVELOPING THE EXPEDITION THAT word of the naturalist's death did not arrive in Europe or reach Steller's family until many months later. Steller's final letter to the Academy became his last will and testament.

We have only a few glimpses of the work Steller planned to do with his materials. We know that he was comparing the anatomy of different birds and fishes. He certainly wondered about migration patterns, life cycles, and the effect of habitat on plant distribution. He had theories to explain the arrival of foxes on Bering Island and of the Itelmen on Kayak Island. He looked to weather conditions, island shape, and orientation to understand the complete absence of trees from the Shumagin Islands. It is as if Darwin had died a year after his voyage on the *Beagle*, many of his materials gathered but his long contemplative period only begun and his conclusions far in the future.

Although Steller did not live long enough to make use of his collections and manuscripts, they have served other scientists. His plants made their way to the Academy of Sciences in St. Petersburg, where Gmelin used them for his four-volume *Flora Sibirica* (*Plants of Siberia*). Demidov sent Carolus Linnaeus, the great Swedish botanist, packets of seeds produced in his greenhouses from Steller's plants. Linnaeus included the plants grown from these seeds in his system of botanical classification and replied sympathetically, "I lament and shall never cease to lament the loss to botanical science of Steller, who during his great journey traversed so many untrodden lands. O merciful God, that you have taken away such a man!" In the Latin of Linnaeus: "O Bone Deus, quod tantum virum eripuisti!"

Carolus Linnaeus

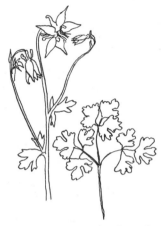

Western Columbine, *Aquilegia formosa*

Krasheninnikov incorporated much of Steller's information, especially his descriptions of fish, in his book *Description of the Land of Kamchatka.*

Over the years, a number of plants and animals have been named after Steller in recognition of his having been the first scientist to collect or describe them. Some species are familiar to us by their English names: Steller's eider, Steller's albatross, Steller's wormwood, Steller's sea cow, Steller's sea lion, and Steller's jay. In other species he is commemorated only by a Latin epithet: *Harrimanella stelleriana* and *Cryptochiton stelleri*. Although, in the past, four genera have been named for him, at present only one small genus found in temperate Asia bears his name, *Stellera.*

Steller had witnessed the last stage of Itelmen culture before its religious traditions were replaced by Christianity. As the Itelmen children began attending Russian schools, the people moved further and further away from their ancestral beliefs and practices. Only recently, since the fall of Soviet communism, have the Itelmen revived some of their ancient customs and ceremonies by drawing on Steller's accounts. They regard him as their most reliable and sympathetic historian.

Twenty years ago, before the Russian archives were opened to scholars outside the Soviet Union, we would have had to end this story with the sad conclusion that, just as Steller had feared when he wrote to the Academy of Sciences from the Demidov estate, his life's work had been scattered and might never be found. But in 1990 Dr. Wieland Hintzsche of the Francke Foundations in Halle recovered most of Steller's journals, long buried in the extensive archives of St. Petersburg. Now, more than 250 years after the great naturalist's death, his journals and letters are being carefully transcribed and edited.

As these and other writings connected with the expedition are published, Georg Steller's personality, his contribution to science, and the beauty of his writing about nature and native peoples will become more widely known and appreciated. For someone so volatile and impatient with his fellow man, so unbuttoned and forthright in many of his descriptions, this long eclipse has at least one redeeming aspect. The timeless qualities of Steller's personality stand out in still higher relief today, attracting editors and translators more sympathetic to his style and observations, than at any earlier time in the last 250 years.

Steller's sea eagle
Haliaeetus pelagicus

Steller's jay
Cyanocitta stelleri

Steller's albatross
Phoebastria albatrus

Steller's sculpin
Myoxocephalus stelleri

Steller's sea lion • *Eumetopias jubatus*

Steller's eider • *Polysticta stelleri*

Steller's sea cow • *Hydrodamalis gigas*

APPENDIX
CONCORDANCE FOR ANIMALS
AND PLANTS MENTIONED IN THE TEXT
By Rudolf Schmid, University of California, Berkeley

Key: Common name used in text (alternate common name used elsewhere) = current Latin name: genus/species (older Latin name) (*plus for plants* family: Latin name, common name)

Abbreviations: subsp., subspecies; var., variety

ANIMALS

(In alphabetical order by common name)

Baikal seal (nerpa) = *Phoca sibirica*

blue fox (Arctic fox, white fox) = *Vulpes lagopus* (or *Alopex lagopus*)

flounder = *Pleuronectes stellatus*

gray heron = *Ardea cinerea* (*Note:* This is the species Steller knew as a child in Windsheim.)

gumboot chiton = *Cryptochiton stelleri*

horned puffin = *Fratercula corniculata*

northern fur seal (sea bear) = *Callorhinus ursinus*

old squaw duck (long-tailed duck, aangitsh) = *Clangula hyemalis*

sea otter = *Enhydra lutris*

spectacled cormorant = *Phalacrocorax perspicillatus* (EXTINCT)

Steller's albatross (short-tailed albatross) = *Phoebastria albatrus*

Steller's eider = *Polysticta stelleri* (*Anas stelleri*)

Steller's jay = *Cyanocitta stelleri*

Steller's sculpin = *Myoxocephalus stelleri*

Steller's sea cow = *Hydrodamalis gigas* (EXTINCT)

Steller's sea eagle = *Haliaeetus pelagicus*

Steller's sea lion (northern sea lion) = *Eumetopias jubatus*

tufted puffin = *Fratercula cirrhata*

PLANTS

(In alphabetical order by common name)

Alaska bellheather (Alaskan mountain heather) = *Harrimanella stelleriana* (Ericaceae, heath family)

American brooklime (American speedwell, beccabunga) = *Veronica americana* (Scrophulariaceae, figwort family)

Arctic gentian = *Gentiana algida* (Gentianaceae, gentian family)

bistort = *Bistorta vivipara* (Polygonaceae, buckwheat family)

bitter cress (bittercress, cuckoo flower) = *Cardamine pratensis* subsp. *angustifolia* and *C. hirsuta* (Brassicaceae/Cruciferae, mustard family)

cloudberry (yellow and black scurvy berries) = *Rubus chamaemorus* (Rosaceae, rose family)

cotton grass (Steller also refers to *gramine Cyperoide* and Cypergrass) = *Eriophorum* species (Cyperaceae, sedge family) (*Note:* This is a sedge, not a true grass.)

crested wheatgrass = *Agropyron cristatum* (Gramineae/Poaceae, grass family)

crowberry = *Empetrum nigrum L.* (Empetraceae, crowberry family)

fragile rockbrake or cliffbrake (Steller's rockbrake) = *Cryptogramma stelleri* (Pteridaceae, maidenhair fern family, brake family)

Kamchatkan fir = *Abies nephrolepis* (Pinaceae, pine family)

Kamchatkan sweet grass (cow parsnip) = *Heracleum lanatum* (Apiaceae/Umbelliferae, carrot family) (*Note:* This is an umbel, not a true grass.)

purple fireweed (fireweed) = *Chamerion angustifolium* subsp. *angustifolium* (Onagraceae, evening primrose family)

salmonberry (salmon berry) = *Rubus spectabilis* var. *spectabilis* (Rosaceae, rose family)

sarana lily (chocolate lily) = *Fritillaria camschatcensis* (Liliaceae, lily family)

scurvy grass (scurvygrass) = *Cochlearia officinalis* (Brassicaceae/Cruciferae, mustard family) (*Note:* This is a mustard, not a true grass.)

sea lungwort = *Mertensia maritima* (Boraginaceae, borage family)

snow rose (snowrose, rosebay) = *Rhododendron chrysanthum* (Ericaceae, heath family)

speedwell (brooklime) = *Veronica stelleri* (Scrophulariaceae, figwort family)

Steller's wormwood = *Artemisia stelleriana* (Asteraceae/Compositae, sunflower family)

upland cranberry (mountain cranberry, lingonberry) = *Vaccinium vitis-idaea* (Ericaceae, heath family)

wintergreen (shinleaf) = *Pyrola minor* (Pyrolaceae, wintergreen family)

no common name (angelica) = *Angelica gmelinii* (Apiaceae/Umbelliferae, carrot family)

no common name = *Lapathum folio cubitali* (Polygonaceae, buckwheat family) (*Note:* probably Rumex arcticus)

REFERENCES

Among the many texts and Web sources consulted, the following were particularly helpful:

Czerepanov, S. K. (Sergei Kirillovich). 1995. *Vascular Plants of Russia and Adjacent States (the Former USSR).* Rev. ed. Cambridge University Press, Cambridge. [Revision of *Plantae vasculares URSS* (1981).]

Golder, F. A. 1922, 1925. *Bering's Voyages: An Account of the Efforts of the Russians to Determine the Relation of Asia and America.* Vol. 1. *The Log Books and Official Reports of the First and Second Expeditions, 1725–1730 and 1733–1742.* Vol. 2. *Steller's Journal of the Sea Voyage from Kamchatka to America and Return on the Second Expedition, 1741–1742.* Stejneger, Leonhard Hess (translator and annotator). American Geographical Society, New York (series: American Geographical Society, research series no. 12).

Web sources: http://plants.usda.gov and www.gifte.de/Giftpflanzen

Steller's jay

Cyanocitta stelleri

Sitka spruce
Picea sitchensis

Fox sparrow
Passerella iliaca

Western hemlock
Tsuga heterophylla

Glaucous-winged gull
Larus glaucescens

TIME LINE
Georg Wilhelm Steller

1709	Born in Windsheim and named Georg Wilhelm Stöller.
1729–34	Stöller attends University of Wittenburg and University of Halle.
1734	Stöller travels from Danzig in Poland to St. Petersburg in Russia, where he changes his name to Steller.
1737	In February, Steller is appointed adjunct to the Second Kamchatka Expedition. He marries Brigitta Helena Messerschmidt, widow of the naturalist Daniel Gottlieb Messerschmidt. Georg and Brigitta Helena travel to Moscow.
1738	Steller's wife remains in Moscow. Steller crosses the Ural Mountains to Siberia.
1739	In January, Steller meets the Academy contingent, Professors Gmelin and Müller, in Yeniseisk in central Siberia. On March 23, he arrives in Irkutsk in Siberia with his artist, Berckhan, his Russian student translator, Gorlanov, and his assistant, Danilov. That summer, Steller explores the Barguzin Mountains.
1740	Steller travels to Kyakhta on the Russian-Chinese border and Yakutsk in Siberia. He goes on to Okhotsk, where he agrees to sail to Kamchatka under Captain Commander Bering.
1740–41	Steller spends nine months traveling throughout the Kamchatka peninsula. He learns cures for scurvy from Kamchadal women shamans.
1741	Steller sails for America on the *St. Peter* with seventy-eight men on board. On July 15, Steller sights the Alaskan shore, and on July 20, both of the ship's boats land on an offshore is-

land, now called Kayak Island. Steller goes ashore. The next day, the *St. Peter* begins its return voyage. On August 29, they reach an island group where Nikita Shumagin dies of scurvy—his was the first death on the voyage. Steller picks antiscorbutic herbs. The first European contact with native Alaskans. On November 6, the *St. Peter* shipwrecks on an island. On December 8, Bering dies. Lieutenant Waxell assumes command.

1742 After the deaths of thirty-two men, the rest recover from scurvy on Bering Island by eating fresh sea mammal meat and herbs recommended by Steller. The crew members build a new ship from the wreckage of the *St. Peter* while Steller walks around the island, observing and writing about the sea mammals. On August 14, he and the crew leave Bering Island in the new, smaller *St. Peter*, reaching Avacha Bay two weeks later.

1743–44 Steller explores the peninsula of Kamchatka, wintering with the fierce Olyutor Koriaks.

1746 On November 12, Steller dies of a fever in Tyumen on his way to St. Petersburg.

1747–69 Publication of Gmelin's four-volume *Flora Sibirica*, incorporating Steller's plant materials.

1751–52 Publication of Gmelin's Siberian diaries.

1755 Publication of Krasheninnikov's *Explorations of Kamchatka* in Russian, including material from Steller's Kamchatkan notebooks.

1774 Publication of *Steller's History of Kamchatka* in German.

1793 First German publication of Steller's journal on the *St. Peter*.

1990 Dr. Wieland Hintzsche discovers Steller's lost journals in St. Petersburg's Academy of Sciences archives.

NOTES

1. *Sonntagskind*: A Sunday's Child

4 **"city of Windsheim":**

Germany as a unified country did not exist when Georg Stöller was born. Instead, there were many small kingdoms and principalities, each ruled by its own prince, king, or bishop. Alongside these stood a few independent cities that swore allegiance only to the Holy Roman Empire. Their citizens established their own forms of government, paid taxes into their own coffers, chose their own religion, and, while perhaps not numerous enough to support a standing army, were prepared to defend their cities themselves.

After 1341, the city of Windsheim (now called Bad Windsheim) formed part of the Holy Roman Empire. It had a small population, perhaps no more than five thousand people. Yet it was protected against the greed and ambition of princes by stone walls and the courage of its citizens.

In 1521, Windsheim became one of the first cities of Europe to embrace the ideas of Martin Luther: its citizens welcomed Protestant preachers and drove out the monks from the Roman Catholic Monastery of St. Augustine. Georg was raised in the Lutheran faith.

4 **"Every subject was taught in Latin":**

In early eighteenth-century Europe, many people never left the place in which they were born. There they spoke the language of their region. But those who wished to communicate with people from other provinces or countries would learn to speak, read, and write Latin as well. It was the professional language of lawyers, philosophers, doctors, ministers, and scientists. Even today much of the vocabulary in these fields is based on Latin. When scientists found a new plant or animal, they described it in

Latin so that they could share their knowledge with learned men and women internationally.

5 "Schoszbach Forest":

The Schoszbach Forest nesting grounds of the gray heron were famous for miles around. Every year there was a heron hunt to the music of a brass band celebrating the occasion. The birds were hunted for their long black head plume, used to adorn both men's and women's hats. While herons are occasionally seen in Windsheim today, they no longer nest in the Schoszbach Forest.

5–6 "rare and unusual plants . . . published floras of the area":

After the Ice Age, the retreating glaciers in the Windsheim valley left behind a special endemic flora, plants that grow only in one particular place, or in one particular time—for example, the flora of the Ural Mountains or of the Devonian period in geology. A flora is also a treatise on such plants.

6 "Francke Foundations":

August Hermann Francke (1663–1727), a Lutheran pastor and one of the first professors at the University of Halle, established an orphanage just outside Halle's city walls. During his lifetime it expanded to include schools for rich and poor alike. There was a school for girls, a Latin school, and a school for the sons of wealthy and noble families. The idea of extending education to both sexes and every social class was very unusual at this time: the successful example of the Francke schools revolutionized the concept of education throughout Europe. Around the schools, a library, a hospital, a pharmacy, a printing office, a bookstore, and gardens sprang up, forming, by 1733, a school town with over two thousand pupils and almost two hundred teachers.

7 "the future unfolded just as Georg had foretold":

In 1788, Elias Reichard wrote and published the account from which I have taken this dialogue. By then all but the last of Georg's predictions for the two friends had come true. Reichard did indeed meet Georg's brother, Augustin, at Nienburg in 1738. Two years later he was appointed professor at the Gymnasium of Altona, advancing by 1754 to the position of rector of the Magdeburg Gymnasium. In 1744, Reichard's father died, but Elias did not reach home in time to be at his deathbed. And finally, as the "von" in their surnames attests, Reichard's two wives—Loudovika von Schwandes and Friderika von Krosigk—were of aristocratic origin. Reichard died on September 18, 1791, at the age of seventy-seven, just a few years short of Steller's prediction.

7–8 "Cabinet of Artifacts and Curiosities":

The cabinets of curiosities of scholars, kings, and amateur collectors were the first European museums. While some were cluttered magpie hoardings of unusual objects, others served as teaching collections for doctors or professors. The cabinet of curiosities at the Francke Foundations was arranged in decorative cases by the painter Gottfried August Gründler (1710–1775) according to the most modern principles of museum arrangement prevailing in 1736, shortly after Georg left Halle. The collection is the earliest cabinet of curiosities still surviving in the cases designed for it in its original location. It has recently been restored after years of war, poverty, and neglect.

Peter the Great returned from his European travels in 1698 determined to rival all other rulers in the formation of scientific and cultural institutions. The anatomical collections he had visited, especially in Holland, inspired Peter to found a cabinet of curiosities in 1713. He issued an edict to the regional governors of his empire demanding that his subjects send any unusual object, from complete mammoth skeletons to two-headed sheep, and threatened heavy penalties for neglecting to forward something of interest. Within a short time, rooms full of curios were accumulating in St. Petersburg. But Peter's instructions were not limited to bizarre natural objects. Examples of native craftsmanship from remote parts of the kingdom were gathered and shipped to St. Petersburg. There were all manner of objects, from sacred tribal masks to Scythian helmets and gold armbands, excavated from grave sites. Everything was displayed in beautiful wooden cases to impress scientists or visiting dignitaries with the wealth and variety of the Czar's empire and the modern scientific approach cultivated by the ruler himself. Peter also purchased great collections from the estates of scientists in Europe.

The intelligent arrangement of collections in cabinets of curiosities helped to define scientific disciplines. What had begun as accumulations of objects for their own sake came, with time, to determine the boundaries of individual studies—conchology, mineralogy, embryology, archaeology, and other sciences—each becoming a distinct field of investigation.

2. Russia's Great Explorations: The First and Second Kamchatka Expeditions

12 "build a ship, the *Fortuna*":

The *Fortuna* was called a *shitik*, a "sewn one," because osiers and leather thongs were used to attach the sideboards to the structure of the ship, rather than the wooden pegs and iron nails that were used to hold most ships together.

13 "the recently formed Academy of Sciences":

After touring and admiring European schools and universities, Peter the Great intended to build institutions modeled upon those that had evolved in Europe and England over several hundred years. He laid plans for Latin schools, a university, and an Academy of Sciences. Brilliant German and French scholars and professors would be recruited for the Academy positions until there were Russians qualified to fill them. The foreign scholars would educate Russian students, preparing them to become teachers in the new Russian schools or to be appointed to the Academy in St. Petersburg. Peter had built up the Russian Navy in the same way and was very satisfied with the result. In addition to their scholarly duties, the academicians were required to stage spectacular firework displays for all important royal celebrations.

In January 1724, Peter signed a general plan founding the Imperial Academy of Sciences in St. Petersburg. Though he died the next year, before the completion of his project, his widow, Catherine I, gave the institution her full support until her death two years later. Peter II, the grandson of Peter the Great by his first wife, came to power in 1727, ruling from Moscow and taking little interest in the Academy. When he died of smallpox in 1730, Empress Anna, daughter of Peter the Great's half brother Ivan V, moved the court back to the more European capital of St. Petersburg. She was Empress when Bering returned from his first mission in 1730, and ruled for the next ten years. In November 1741, Empress Elizabeth, daughter of Peter the Great, seized power. She gave the directorship of the Academy to a close relation, excluding the Germans from control.

14 "Bering . . . had beautiful new maps":

There has been a long debate as to the success and true purpose of Bering's First Kamchatka Expedition of 1725–30. Those who claimed that the primary goals were the establishment of a trade route, a northeast passage, along the northern Siberian coast and the discovery of America considered the expedition a failure. But the elevation of Bering to Captain Commander and the fact that he was placed in charge of the Second Kamchatka Expedition support the view of Professor Carol Urness and others that the making of maps of the Russian Empire for political and trade purposes was the chief objective of the first expedition. It is certainly true that when the time came for the Second Kamchatka Expedition, there was no need to redraw the excellent maps made during the first.

14 "The Senate instructed Bering":

In 1711, Peter the Great founded the Administrative Senate, based upon the Swedish model. It had eleven members selected by the Czar— one for each ministry. The War Minister represented the Army, the Admiralty Minister represented the Navy, and so on. In 1722, a table of ranks was published so that precedence could be determined at any gathering, correct forms of address could be used between inferior and superior persons, and lines of command could be established. Captain Commander Bering ranked fifth in the Admiralty hierarchy, the highest class for those who went to sea. But the Academy of Sciences was not established until 1725; its members and administration stood outside the table of ranks. This posed a problem during the Second Kamchatka Expedition. The naval officers and the professors from the Academy, and the local governors, who were often Army officers and whose rank was defined by the Army, were constantly jostling for position because the professors' rank was not clearly defined. If the professors were above the officers in status, they could make demands; if they were beneath the officers, they could only make requests. And who should have the best housing when both professors and naval officers happened to be in the same town together? Only after several years of correspondence did the Senate send word that the professors were to be treated as though their rank was level 9. Both Chirikov and Spangberg were above them at level 6, Bering still higher at level 5. But as the professors were allowed to make their own plans, informing rather than consulting Bering, they came to regard him as merely first among equals: their realm was independent of the Captain Commander. Steller, however, was an adjunct, and as such subservient—or so they felt.

In St. Petersburg, Bering was ordered to provide river and seagoing transportation for the professors. The Senate instructed the professors to perform the tasks they chose to do and coordinate their work with Bering.

The senior secretary of the Administrative Senate and head of the Geodetic Service was Ivan K. Kirilov. As a cartographer, he prepared the first atlas of Russia, which appeared in 1734. His memorandum stated the Senate's objectives for the Second Kamchatka Expedition:

> (1) to find out for certain whether it is possible to pass from the Arctic Ocean to the Kamchatka or Southern Ocean sea [now known as the Bering Sea] (I hope ultimately in light of the investigations of several people that this is so); (2) to reach from Kamchatka the very shores of America at some unknown place about 45 degrees of longitude; (3) to go from Kamchatka to Japan, between which the distance is only ten degrees of north latitude; (4) on that voyage and everywhere to search for new lands and islands not yet conquered and to bring them under subjection; (5) to search for metals and minerals; (6) to make various astronomical observations both on land and sea and to find accurate longitude and latitude; (7) to write a history of the old and the new, as well as natural history, and other matters.

16 **"He chose to investigate the archives of all Siberian towns":**
While Professor Müller was searching through the archives of

Yakutsk in 1736, he came upon an account written by a Russian merchant, Semyon Dezhnev. The merchant described sailing from the Arctic Sea in 1648, through what we now call the Bering Strait, and down the eastern coast of Kamchatka, thus establishing almost a hundred years before Bering's first expedition that Asia and America are not connected. Because Dezhnev's report had never been sent on to the government in Moscow, it remained unknown until Müller's discovery.

18 "Some of the governors of the towns along the way were helpful":

Sometimes governors went to extreme lengths to protect themselves from the demands of the expedition members. When Müller went to Tomsk in 1740, he found the archives strangely lacking in older documents. On questioning the authorities, he was told that a recent fire had destroyed everything. The truth was even more upsetting. The *voyevoda*, the chief administrative and judicial officer of the province, had thrown all the older documents in the river Tom just before Müller arrived, hoping the exacting professor and his entourage would swiftly move on to some other town.

19 "his wife, Anna":

Little is known about the women who joined their husbands on the expedition. No journal or correspondence seems to have survived with the exception of a clutch of sixteen undelivered letters to relatives and friends in St. Petersburg from Vitus Bering and his wife, Anna Christina, in Okhotsk. They were discovered by Natasha Okhotina Lind and Peter Ulf Møller in an archive in Moscow, their wax seals still unbroken, more than 250 years after they were written. The letters were first published in Copenhagen in 1997.

Anna and Vitus Bering left their two older sons behind in Tallinn, in the care of an old family friend, so that the children might receive a good European education. Their two younger offspring, Anton, born in 1730, and Anushka, born the next year, and Anna's young nephew, Johann Lund, traveled with the Berings across Siberia to Yakutsk in 1734. In an attempt to preserve something of their comfortable, elegant St. Petersburg way of life, Anna brought her table linens, porcelain, silver, and, amazingly, her clavichord across Siberia all the way to the Sea of Okhotsk.

Bering established his headquarters in Yakutsk in October 1734. For the next three years he directed operations from this remote outpost. Although he and his men accomplished a tremendous amount of construction and provisioning during this time, to some it seemed that the Berings were lingering in Yakutsk rather than moving on to the more rigorous part of the expedition, the voyage to Kamchatka and America. Bering had his detractors among the professors, government spies, and local officials who were forced to accommodate him. They pointed to the couple's enjoyment of the pleasures of the sleigh, their distillation of brandy, and their trading of such alcoholic spirits for valuable furs as signs of dissipation and neglect of duty.

When Bering eventually led his contingent on to Okhotsk, his wife and children made plans for the return trip to St. Petersburg. But on hearing that her husband was ill, Anna traveled with her children by boat and by horse to nurse him back to health in Okhotsk. We learn from Anna Bering's letters that she lost her way on the journey from Yakutsk over the Yablonoi Mountains. She confided in one letter: "My Bering had absolutely no idea where in the wilderness I had strayed, which made him slightly ill because a great number of my horses ran away, some succumbed, my children and I were in danger of dying from hunger and exposure."

Shortly before Bering's ships were ready to sail, Anna and the children set out again in seven carts with their eleven chests holding furs, silver, Chinese silks, and the clavichord. They arrived in Moscow in March 1742; six months later they went on to St. Petersburg.

20 "the professors had gallows set up":

In Siberia, the people would be all too aware of the significance of building gallows. Punishment and execution in Russia, as elsewhere in Europe and Asia at this time, were public spectacles attended by every level of society. In August 1737, a meeting of the Academy of Sciences was canceled so that members need not miss a public execution of street robbers. In Tobolsk, Steller watched the decapitation of a father and son convicted of counterfeiting, and in Irkutsk, he witnessed the burning of another criminal. Knouting and slitting the criminal's nostrils before sending him off to Siberia were standard punishments.

3. On to Russia: Stöller Becomes Steller

21 **"Most cities begin as small settlements":**

The land on which St. Petersburg stands was originally settled by Slavic tribes. In the tenth century these tribes joined the feudal state of Kievan Rus. The river Neva, flowing into the Baltic Sea, had been the most important trade route between Russia and the rest of Europe for a long while. In the early seventeenth century the kingdom of Sweden seized this estuary land, and in 1700 the Great Northern War began between Russia and Sweden. In 1703, when Peter the Great succeeded in winning back these lands, he immediately built a fortress to protect them from future invasion. This was the beginning of the construction of St. Petersburg, the new capital of Russia.

August Ludwig von Schlözer, a Nordic historian who came to St. Petersburg in 1761 to act as assistant to Professor Müller, gave his impressions of the young city:

> Much that in other places is beautiful, but small, is here splendid and grand; much that elsewhere is great, is here colossal, gigantic . . . What a multitude of human races, nationalities and languages! . . . Here meet Asia and Europe. Armenians, Kalmucks, Bukharians, etc., people—possibly without exception—from *all* parts of our continent. Look around in the most populous streets, what a variety among the men in physiognomy, in costume!

23 **"changed his name to Steller":**   ШТЕ ЛЛЕР

The spelling of names had yet to be standardized in the eighteenth century, particularly when problems of transliteration—changing from one alphabet to another—were involved. When Martin Pedersen Spangberg enlisted in the Russian Navy in 1720, he signed his name M. P. Spangberg. On documents after 1741, his signature reads M. P. Spangenberg. In the English-language version of the *Great Soviet Encyclopedia*, his

entry is under Martyn Petrovich Shpanberg. Other forms of his name include Spannberg, Spanberg, and Spangsberg. His most recent biographer
uses a spelling unknown to Spangberg himself but preferred by an exist-
ing Danish family of the same name. In Russian, his middle name was
Petrovich, while in Danish it was Petersen or Pedersen; all three names
mean "son of Peter." Sometimes his first name is spelled Marten; in Denmark it was Morten.

24 "Steller helped the Swiss botanist Dr. Johann Amman":

While visiting Sir Hans Sloane's Museum in London, Johann Amman
(1707–41), a brilliant young Swiss botanist with an international reputation, happened to meet Professor Müller, who was abroad seeking promising young men to bring back to St. Petersburg. In 1733, Amman was
recruited by Müller to the Academy of Sciences, where he soon became
professor of botany. When Steller applied for the position of adjunct on
the Second Kamchatka Expedition, he was examined, and found to be
fully qualified, by Amman.

24 "catalog its herbarium":

An herbarium is a collection of plants, preserved by being pressed
and dried. The specimens are mounted on sheets of paper on which is
written the date and location of the gathering and sometimes other rele-
vant information (scent, peculiarities of form as a result of location, local
medicinal use, pollinating insects seen on the plant, and so on). The
mounted specimens are then classified by whatever system is in use at the
time and arranged in protective cases.

The first specimen to be gathered and named of a particular plant is
called the type specimen; it becomes the official standard by which the
species is defined, the judge of last resort in cases of dispute.

25 "the Academy's superb library":

In the eighteenth century, large or costly books were regularly published and sold by subscription over time. Books with color plates could
be published in fascicles, or installments, a few plates at a time with their
descriptive text. When enough fascicles had been published to make a
volume, the printer would issue a title page, and the purchaser would

have the sections bound together in decorative paper, leather, or vellum covers. Only then would the book be ready for the shelf.

The size of a book was named and determined by the dimensions of the paper on which its pages were printed and by the format or number of times that whole sheet of paper was then folded. If the sheet was folded only once (as with a newspaper), the book was called a folio; if twice, a quarto (making four leaves with eight pages); three foldings made an octavo (eight leaves, sixteen pages). Further foldings produced still smaller books with more pages.

In Steller's time, color illustrations were usually made by applying watercolor to engravings printed in black and white. The colorist would have a model illustration to work from, but inevitably no two copies were exactly alike.

26 "Terrible bouts of fever":

The fevers of Siberia were notorious for their intensity. In the Russian popular imagination, a person suffering from a fever was thought to be possessed by evil spirits. Icons, amulets, prayers, or charms were commonly used in efforts to stave off infection or hasten recovery. One type of illness, a *triasavitsy*, or "shaking fever," was traditionally attributed to the twelve daughters of Herod. The healer or priest would try to banish a *tri-*

asavitsy by calling the twelve sisters by name. In one prayer-charm collected in the nineteenth century, St. Sisinnius, the saint commonly invoked in cases of fever, asks the accursed sisters to identify themselves. As
they respond, each name is recognizable as an aspect of fever: chills, burning, shivering, wheezing, swelling, deafness, jaundice, and the sensation
that one's bones are being broken as if by a strong storm.

In this popular icon, St. Sisinnius sits in his robes on a mountainside
while Herod's daughters stand at the edge of a stream. (Russians associated fevers with water of all kinds, flowing, stagnant, salt, or fresh.)

27 **"he married Brigitta Helena von Boeckler":**
Messerschmidt had first met Brigitta Helena on his way back from
his travels, when she was a girl of thirteen living with her father, an
Army officer stationed in Solikamsk. Messerschmidt had long conversations with the father and wrote poetry for the daughter.

4. Steller's Journey Begins
33 **"the Russians' differing treatment of various Siberian
peoples":**
In Steller's time the inhabitants of Siberia were a rough-and-tumble
assortment. There were the established families, like the Demidovs,
whose wealth was derived from mines and foundries and from the cannons and munitions they provided for the wars of Peter the Great. Then
there were wealthy aristocrats exiled from the court for real or imagined
political offenses, biding their time until a new ruler came to power and
needed their services in St. Petersburg. Criminals of lowly social status
were sent to the far east, their noses slit for easy recognition. Local tribesmen and nomadic reindeer herders were plagued by tax collectors: instead
of gathering food for their families, the native people were forced to
spend much of their time hunting fur-bearing animals to pay their *yasak*,
fur taxes. There were Russian peasants, too, engaged in farming the land
taken from the native Siberians. There were very few serfs, most of whom
were working in Russian Orthodox monasteries. And threading their way
through all these groups were unpredictable bands of roving Cossacks engaged in plunder on an alarming scale. Müller describes entering a silent
village where only a week before Cossacks had murdered every man,

woman, and child and laid the village to waste. For protection there were garrisons with soldiers and Army officers.

The borders were patrolled by customs officials so that the lucrative trade in furs—sables, foxes, ermines, and squirrels—could be regulated and taxed as goods passed from one province into another.

33 "They wrote to the Senate":

Through Bering's efforts, there was a monthly postal service from Okhotsk to Tobolsk and weekly service from Tobolsk to St. Petersburg. The professors were allowed to send both private and academic correspondence without payment. All letters went first to the Senate, where they were translated into Russian if they were in Latin or a foreign language. Private correspondence was scrutinized and censored: no mention of the accomplishments or discoveries of the expedition was permitted to go on to private persons.

37 "miserable government huts":

Gmelin had made the same trip four years earlier and described the government huts in these terms:

> We stopped at a *zimovye* [a winter hut kept by the government for accomodation of travelers], where we had to feed the horses and eat dinner . . . As we entered the room we felt as if we had come into a den of murderers, so black and dark and ugly did it appear, and the fellow who lived there looked also almost like a murderer. We were inside quite a while without receiving an answer from him, and because of the darkness, which changed the day into night, we lost sight of him repeatedly. Besides, it was difficult to believe that one man was living alone by himself, in such an out-of-the-way place. However, all my conjectures were off the mark. That the fellow did not answer us was due to his being deaf, and in addition he was so old that he had to sit down frequently in a corner to rest. The Tatars at Ust Kemtchisk had hired him to live here during the winter and to bring in as much firewood and hay as might be necessary for the travelers.

5. The Barguzin Mountains

42 "the vast and mysterious Lake Baikal":

Lake Baikal covers an area of about 12,000 square miles and contains one-fifth of the fresh water on earth. It lies in the slowly widening gap between two tectonic plates and as a result is more than a mile deep in places. Hydrothermal vents support life-forms usually associated with saltwater habitats, such as large mushroom-shaped sponges. Some two thousand species live in the lake, at least twelve hundred of which are endemic. Living creatures exist even at the greatest depths, where oxygen is circulated by mysterious tides. Lake Baikal is twenty to thirty million years old, the most ancient lake on earth.

Müller and Gmelin had risked their lives and lost much of their baggage during a stormy four-day crossing of Lake Baikal in September 1735. The local people felt the professors deserved their fate. They had not made offerings of coins before the voyage and had called Baikal a lake instead of the Holy Sea. What else could they expect after such irreverence?

47 "the market town of Kyakhta":

The border town of Kyakhta was established in 1728 as a meeting place for Chinese and Russian merchants. The town was divided in two, one half for each nation. Eventually, a Russian Orthodox church was built in the middle of the Siberian side, mirroring the Chinese temple standing in the center of the Mongolian side (all of Mongolia then being part of China). Tall sharpened logs surrounded the settlement as a palisade. The Chinese brought silks, tobacco, porcelain, tea, powdered sugar, and paper to trade for Russian woolens, linens, leather goods, tinware, and— secretly, but most profitably—all sorts of animal furs.

47 "his fortune told during a traditional shamanistic ceremony":

Native peoples of northeastern Siberia soon became self-conscious and secretive about their religious beliefs under the scrutiny of outside observers such as Messerschmidt and Müller. This was particularly true of the faith they had in their shamans, the healers and religious leaders of their communities.

In the twentieth century, the Communist government, in its effort to eradicate religion in the Soviet Union, tried to eliminate all of the shamans of Siberia. In 2001, Piers Vitebsky, a British anthropologist, attended a healing séance given by the last practicing Tungus shaman in Siberia. The shaman's costume and drum that he describes in *The Reindeer People* is reminiscent of those depicted by the artists of the Second Kamchatka Expedition and very likely similar to that of the Sakha shaman who told Steller's fortune in Yakutsk.

The shaman sat on a rectangular mat made from the brown head-fur of two wild male reindeer, the slits of the eye-holes and antler-holes sealed with the white fur of a male domestic reindeer. Patches of wolverine, bear, and lynx were sewn around the border with thread of wild reindeer sinew. His robe was made from tanned elk hide, processed with a dye obtained from the inner bark of an alder tree, and embroidered with a brass sun as well as iron representations of the shaman's own skeleton and of his animal and bird spirits. Every item was laden with meaning. From the shaman's waist hung tassels embroidered with tufts of fur gathered from a reindeer's throat, the seat of its soul, in such a way that not a single hair was scattered or lost. His headdress was made of two crossed strips of decorated cloth, representing the four corners of the universe, from which a fringe of fur tassels covered his eyes to conceal the ordinary world as he made his voyage of insight into another reality.

The four struts of the cross-piece on the inside of his flat drum likewise represented the four directions. The shaman himself stood at the centre of the universe, which for the duration of this ritual would be located in the village hall of Sebyan. The inside of the drum was ornamented with iron models of his helping spirits: an eider-duck and a bear. A pair of bear's ears would enable him to hear the speech of spirits, and twelve pine cones represented each of the levels of the cosmos to which he was qualified to fly.

7. Captain Martin Spangberg:
Okhotsk, the Kuril Islands, and Japan

60 *"yasak* (tax payment)":

Yasak, or fur tax, was a levy that each adult male native tribesman in
Siberia paid to the Russian imperial government with pelts of foxes,
sables, ermines, or squirrels.

62 "Spangberg's new orders":

In December 1742, with an eye to assuming the leadership of the expedition, Captain Chirikov wrote to the Admiralty, attempting to de-
stroy Captain Spangberg's reputation by repeating false rumors about his
activities in Okhotsk. He accused his rival of trading homemade vodka
for furs, collecting *yasak* for his own gain, and refusing to pay his workers. He suggested that Spangberg's wife, who traveled with him, was notorious for selling Chinese tobacco to native women at great profit. Major
General Pisarev's accusations added fuel to the fire. Spangberg wrote a
declaration to the Admiralty stating that the allegations were false, but
the confidence of the Admiralty was shaken. In 1744, Chirikov was chosen to succeed Bering as supreme commander of the expedition.

After confirming his Kuril Island charts on his third voyage in 1742,
Spangberg returned to Okhotsk and Yakutsk. There he became embroiled
in the question of justice for the native Yakut herdsmen, who had lost
many horses during the expedition, just as Steller was to support the
cause of the Itelmen two years later.

Unfortunately for Spangberg, his archenemy, Pisarev, was recalled
and reinstated in St. Petersburg under the new regime of Empress Elizabeth, Peter the Great's daughter, who came to power in November 1741.
Pisarev did everything he could to prevent Spangberg from receiving the
advancement and recognition he deserved. There were a number of out-
standing complaints against Spangberg that could not be resolved without testimony from the aggrieved parties, who were still in Siberia. We
know that one earlier accusation was written under the encouragement of
Pisarev; probably others had the same origin. Spangberg could not rise in
rank before judgment had been given. As a result, for the rest of his life
he never rose above the rank of captain. When Spangberg returned to St.
Petersburg in 1745 without official permission, he was degraded in rank

and placed under arrest until 1747. In 1749, twenty-eight people died when a ship under his command capsized without warning as Spangberg sailed her out of the harbor of Arkhangelsk on her maiden voyage. Spangberg was placed under house arrest until 1752, when he was finally declared innocent of any wrongdoing. He continued to serve in the Navy until he died, still a captain, on September 15, 1761.

8. The Volcanic Wilderness of Kamchatka

65 "Steller met Krasheninnikov for the first time":

After leaving Kamchatka, Krasheninnikov slowly made his way back to St. Petersburg, joining Gmelin en route. They arrived in the capital in February 1743. There the Academy rewarded him for his grueling years in Kamchatka. He became an adjunct to the Academy in 1745 and a professor of botany in 1750. The Academy allowed Krasheninnikov to use Steller's Kamchatka manuscripts when preparing his own history of Kamchatka. Krasheninnikov died in St. Petersburg in February 1755, just before the publication of his book *Explorations of Kamchatka*.

65 " 'my Cossack' ":

Sometimes the term *Cossack* refers to a member of the tribe from the Russian steppes, famous for their horsemanship, who were the forerunners in Russia's conquest of Siberia and Kamchatka. Occasionally it stands for a government representative sent out as a sort of posse to round up Itelmen for some nefarious purpose, and two or three times Steller refers to his servant, Toma, as "my Cossack" because he had been a member of the Siberian militia.

65 "the beautiful new harbor of Avacha Bay"

Avacha Bay, on the eastern coast of Kamchatka, was a deep, sheltered body of water with a sandy floor. It never froze over completely, so ships could break through the ice and leave in the early spring, lengthening their sailing season. In August 1739, a year before sailing from Okhotsk, Bering sent first mate Ivan Yelagin, second mate Vasily Khmetevski, who would later play an important role in Steller's life, and a few sailors to determine the best site for a settlement and harbor within the confines of Avacha Bay. There the men prepared for Bering's arrival by building storerooms, barracks, and headquarters. Bering named his new town Petropavlovsk after his two ships, the *St. Peter* and the *St. Paul*. Captain Spangberg's son helped to construct a lighthouse marking the entrance to the new harbor, which still stands there today. After enumerating the many fine qualities of the place, Waxell concluded with the ultimate praise a sailor could give: "In a nutshell, this is the best harbour I have seen in all my days."

PETROPAVLOVSK-1740
Adapted from a map drawn by
Ivan Yelagin

1 Traveling church
2 Warehouse
3 Powder house
4 Captain Commander
5 Captain Chirikov
7 Steller & de la Croyère
9 Lieutenant Waxell
13 Blacksmith shop
14 Medical Quarters
15 Guard house
17 Native Kamchadal earthern hut
18 Native summer houses
19 Bath house
20 Freshwater spring

66 *"History of Kamchatka"*

Steller's *History of Kamchatka* was not published until 1774. It was pieced together from his Kamchatka notebooks by a member of the Academy of Sciences, J. B. Scherer.

78 " 'A decoction of scrub pine, called *slanets*' ":

When the famous British explorer Captain James Cook sailed into the seaport of Petropavlovsk, Kamchatka, in 1778, he took on board barrels of *slanets*, a drink made by soaking a particular dwarf pine, as one way to protect his men against scurvy. In his ship's log Cook wrote that *slanets* was recommended to him by a leader of the Itelmen who said that Bering had told him about it. It is more likely that the leader had heard about *slanets* from Steller, whom he associated with Bering.

9. Avacha Bay: Steller Signs On to the *St. Peter*

82 "The *St. Peter*'s officers":

Some of the men who volunteered to join the expedition were temporarily raised to officer status. As officers, they could not be whipped or beaten as punishment. While the promotion was officially only for the duration of the expedition, most of the officers retained their rank throughout their careers. Lieutenant Waxell was an officer of this kind.

As a means of attracting men to serve on the expedition, the Senate offered double pay to the soldiers and sailors who volunteered in St Petersburg. The men who joined in Siberia were not entitled to this extra payment.

83 "one of the two ship's logs"

The ship's logbook was the most important document written during a voyage. It contained a complete running record of the date, weather, phase of the moon, location of the ship, depth of the water, health of the crew, encounters with other ships or native peoples, and descriptions or drawings of any coast they might come upon. Meetings of officers or crew and the decisions they reached were also carefully noted. At the end of a voyage, maps were drawn, a final report was written, and pensions given to widows and children of anyone who had died in the line of duty—all based upon the ship's logbook. The captain of the ship made certain it was written every day without fail. On the *St. Peter* two logs were written up daily, and Steller privately kept his own journal as well.

While the logbook was a public, official record of the voyage, Steller's journal was both a scientific and an intimate, personal account, not intended for publication. In his journal Steller gave vent to his frustrations with irony and sarcasm. He vowed to take revenge by ignoring the welfare of those who teased and despised him. Nonetheless, he dutifully attended to everyone on board, as best he could under the circumstances. He had a hot temper but a warm heart, and his religion would not allow him to abandon his fellow man. Steller's journal records conversations he witnessed, actions and attitudes of the other men, and, of course, everything he could observe in the natural world from the deck of the ship. The excerpts relating to the voyage printed here come from one or another of the two English translations of Steller's journal and from his *De Bestiis Marinis*.

10. They Set Sail for America
86 "Delisle's map had led them astray":

Before the Second Kamchatka Expedition, and Captain James Cook's voyages thirty years later, there were large unknown areas on the maps of the world. Could a ship pass along the northern coast of Siberia? How far was America from Asia? Was there anything in between? Not every cartographer or naturalist relied exclusively on his own observations. Several times in his account of Kamchatka, Steller mentions animals that others claimed to have seen, usually with some bizarre characteristic, but as he himself has not encountered them, he refuses to accept his informant's statement as fact. In Steller's time, science and its methods were still in the process of gaining ascendance over hearsay and imagination. Delisle's infuriatingly unscientific chart, with its imaginary landmass harkened back to a time when filling in the blank portions of a map was more important than recording observed truth.

In his account, Waxell wrote of unreliable charts and maps:

I think it would be only reasonable were such unknown lands first to be explored before they are trumpeted abroad as being the coasts of Yezo or de Gama, for unless such investigations are first undertaken, many a good sailor-man will be most unwarrantably deceived. Those who produce uncertain things of that kind would do better to hold their peace, or, if they must exercise imagination and speculation, let them keep the results to themselves and not put them into the hands of others. I know that I am writing all too much about this matter, but I can hardly tear myself away from it, for my blood still boils whenever I think of the scandalous deception of which we were the victims.

89 " 'a treat to chocolate' ":

Chocolate, sipped from finely decorated porcelain cups, was a rare and expensive luxury in Russia at this time. It was a drink for grownups, not for children. To make sure the cocoa was not mixed with cheaper ingredients, purchasers bought chocolate with only a small part of the processing completed. Servants prepared cocoa at home by grating or grinding the chocolate nibs and adding sugar. Then the cocoa, mixed with hot water, was beaten for a long time with a special wooden instrument, breaking up the cocoa butter, which floated to the surface, and creating the beautiful froth that indicated a well-made cup of cocoa.

Carolus Linnaeus, a chocolate lover, gave the genus the name *Theobroma*, from the Greek, meaning "food of the gods."

93 "a native raspberry":

The unknown species of raspberry was the salmonberry, *Rubus spectabilis*.

94 "Steller's jay":

Steller's jay and the blue jay depicted in Mark Catesby's *Natural History of Carolina, Florida and the Bahama Islands*, the "newest account" referred to by Steller, are different species within the exclusively American genus *Cyanocitta*.

94 " 'An iron kettle, a pound of tobacco' ":

Fifty years after Steller landed on Kayak Island, Joseph Billings, an Englishman sailing under orders from Catherine II of Russia, led an expedition to the southern coast of Alaska. An inhabitant of Kayak Island recounted a childhood memory to Officer Gavriil Sarychev, who commanded one of the vessels on the expedition. Sarychev wrote:

> In 1790, when the Billings expedition visited this island one of
> the old natives said that "he remembered that when he was a boy
> a ship had been close into the bay on the west side of the island
> and had sent a boat on shore; but on its approaching land the na-
> tives all ran away. When the ship sailed, they returned to their
> hut and found in their subterraneous storeroom some glass beads,
> leaves (tobacco), an iron kettle, and something else."

11. Return Voyage: Kayaks and Death

98 "succumbing to scurvy":

Until the middle of the eighteenth century, time was a greater peril
than distance on long sea voyages. After about three months without
some form of vitamin C, human beings inevitably began suffering from
scurvy. On Bering's ship this had become evident by the time they
reached the Shumagin Islands on their way home.

Scurvy was a rare disease before 1450, when ships were small and
could travel only short distances without taking on fresh supplies. But as
ships became larger and more seaworthy, they could be away from port
for longer periods of time. The sailors had to be supplied with foods that
would not spoil, and came to depend upon salted meats, dried vegetables,
and crackers. With this development came the scourge of scurvy. In the
1498 logbook of Vasco da Gama we find a complete picture of the disease. He describes first the puffy gums painfully covering the teeth
and the patient's shortness of breath, then the violet spots on the skin and
the swollen paralyzed limbs, followed by death. However, the progress
of the disease was immediately halted and in fact reversed when he and
his crew met a trading ship laden with oranges and they were able to
add citrus fruits to their diet. Almost overnight the men's symptoms
vanished.

People who live in temperate or tropical places have a steady supply
of green vegetables and fruits containing vitamin C, but those who dwell
in northern climates, with long, cold winters and extended periods with-

out such foods, have had to discover ways to supplement their diets. Potatoes became one important source of the vitamin once they had been brought to Europe from the New World.

The amount of vitamin C in foods is reduced by exposure to heat. But when fish is eaten nearly raw, as it was in the Pacific Northwest, it contains enough vitamin C to keep a person healthy. Steller mentions raw fish as one of the foods recommended by the women shamans among the Itelmen as a cure for scurvy, that is, an antiscorbutic.

Steller and the crew of the *St. Peter* were not the first scurvy sufferers to benefit from the advice of native peoples. In 1535, when the French explorer Jacques Cartier and his crew wintered on an island in the frozen St. Lawrence River in Quebec, with his three ships locked in the ice, almost every sailor suffered from scurvy. They were saved by a passing band of Indians who taught them how to make an infusion from the bark and leaves of a certain tree. The native women instructed the captain to drink the brew and use the dregs as a poultice on affected arms and legs. Within eight days the men had recovered their health and strength. However, when other Frenchmen wintered in the same location only seven years later, the knowledge of which tree to use had been lost, and many died.

The Scottish naval doctor James Lind (1716–94) is the most famous person in the history of scurvy. He carried out the first controlled trial of nutrition in 1746, giving different daily treatments to six pairs of scurvy-stricken men. He concluded that "oranges and lemons were the most effectual remedies for this distemper at sea." That citrus fruits were curative had been known for over two hundred years; Lind's contribution was to prove that cider, vitriol, vinegar, salt water, and a medicinal paste of garlic, mustard seed, and other materials were not effective cures. In 1753, he published a 456-page treatise devoted to the history of scurvy and its treatment. It was, however, almost fifty years before Lind's recommendation—handing out citrus fruits to sailors—was officially put into effect. In the meantime, Captain James Cook and other responsible captains took matters into their own hands by setting a good example in their own diet and by encouraging their men to eat fruits and vegetables whenever they were available.

Before the isolation of vitamin C in the 1930s, the cause of scurvy remained a mystery. Diet, damp air, unclean surroundings, and contagion through contact with afflicted fellow sailors had all been considered possible sources of the disease.

100 "a Chukchi interpreter"

In his account of the expedition, Waxell describes the role played by Khitrov's interpreter when they were stranded on the island:

> When the crew of the yawl from their little island saw us getting under canvas, they thought that we were putting out to sea. Then mist and darkness came and they could see us no more. When that happened they were in despair, believing that they must abandon all hope of being rescued. Their interpreter, who was a Chukchi, seeing how unhappy they were, sought to give them fresh courage by telling them that there was no need to despair, for those on the ship were honourable and fine men who assuredly would not leave them in the lurch. Even though the ship were compelled to stand out to sea, she would still come back again; and if they were compelled to remain some time on the island, that did not mean that they would starve to death, since there was sea-cabbage there, and an abundance of seaweed that had been washed up; that was good to eat, you could keep yourself alive on it . . . With that comfort my friends had to console themselves and take patience, for better was not to be had; and with that they went to bed under the open sky. He who could sleep, slept; and he who could not, wept till he was tired of weeping, and then he too fell asleep.

103 "to retrieve Khitrov and his men":

The *St. Peter* landed on only a few of the fifty islands that make up the archipelago now known as the Shumagin Islands. The watering place where Nikita Shumagin died is now named Nagai Island. Khitrov went first to Turner Island, then on to Nagai, where he stayed for five days until rescued.

103 "Khitrov took the lead in his hand":

A ship's lead is a heavy lead weight tied to a line that is marked with bits of cloth or leather at measured intervals. The line is unwound into the water until the weight strikes the ocean floor, and then brought back to the surface and the number of markers counted to determine the depth of the water. In this way a harbor floor can be charted and safe anchorages established.

12. A Devastating Voyage: Scurvy and Williwaws

112 "williwaws lashing the sails":

A williwaw is a sudden violent gust of cold land air, common along mountainous coasts of high latitudes.

13. Kamchatka or a Barren Island?

124 "Gerhard Friedrich Müller":

Professor Müller was recalled to St. Petersburg in 1739, but his journey home was prolonged when he caught pneumonia in Turinsk. He married a doctor's widow who had nursed him back to health. Under her care he recuperated in the Ural Mountains before continuing on to St. Petersburg in 1743. By then Müller estimated that he had traveled twenty-four thousand miles throughout Siberia during his ten years on the expedition. He returned to the Academy of Sciences with enough material to keep him busily at work on maps, articles, and books for the next thirty-five years. Müller wrote the Siberian volume for a history of Russia.

Although he honored the Academy, Russian scholarship, and the secrecy demanded by the government, Müller's loyalty to Russia was regularly called into question—he remained, after all, a German. In 1750, his rank was reduced to adjunct and his salary cut by two-thirds for drafting a public lecture in which he intended to observe that the Russians were named by the Finns and conquered and enslaved by the Swedes during their early history—the matter remains in dispute to this day. The lecture was never delivered, and most printed copies were destroyed. Six months later he regained his full professorship.

Müller died in Moscow in 1783 at the age of seventy-eight, having spent the last years of his life working in the government archives—and avoiding controversy. While de la Croyère and Gmelin had their portraits drawn and engraved, the only known representation of Gerhard Müller is a silhouette.

14. Bering Island
129 "named the place Bering Island"

Bering Island and, to the southeast, the much smaller Copper Island (named in the late eighteenth century for the copper deposits discovered there), with two islets, form the Commander Islands. They lie beyond the westernmost tip of the Aleutian chain about 110 miles east of Kamchatka.

133 "Sava Starodubtsov":

When the carpenter Sava Starodubtsov returned to Siberia, he was made a nobleman upon the recommendation of Sven Waxell, in gratitude for the crucial role he had played in constructing the new *St. Peter* on Bering Island.

15. Sea Eagles and Sea Cows: The Natural History of Bering Island
139 "sea cow, or northern manatee":

In 1882, Leonhard Stejneger, Steller's biographer, went to Bering Island, where he collected enough bones to form complete sea cow skeletons for the Museum of Comparative Zoology at Harvard University and the Smithsonian Institution in Washington, D.C. In St. Petersburg, there is a third skeleton, preserved along with the chewing plates Steller brought back from Bering Island.

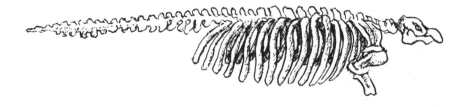

140 "the verge of extinction"

By the end of the eighteenth century the number of sea otters and fur seals had been drastically reduced by Russian hunting. In an effort to restore the populations, the Russians declared a four-year moratorium on fur seal hunting in 1805. After that they instituted a carefully monitored quota system. In 1834, the Russian American Company stopped sea otter hunting for twelve years, after which there was a strict annual limit.

But these restraints were abandoned after the United States purchased Alaska in 1867. It was not until 1911 that an international conservation effort was begun. The Marine Mammal Protection Act (1972) established a commission to encourage international research and conservation of all marine mammals. The Endangered Species Act (1973) listed the southern sea otters as threatened. As a result, they cannot be killed, collected, or wounded, and it is illegal to buy, sell, or possess any part of the animal. There are, however, continuing disputes between fishermen and conservationists, and in recent years the number of sea otters has been in decline.

16. A Safe Return to Kamchatka

148 "The new *St. Peter*":

Although the *St. Peter* had been cobbled together by shipwrecked sailors on a barren island, at the end of her voyage she was still considered seaworthy. During the next twelve years she was used as a trading ship and as a vessel to carry sea otter hunters on expeditions back to the Commander Islands. Eventually, she was wrecked on the coast of Kamchatka, then restored just sufficiently to make a dangerous journey back to Okhotsk in 1754, never to sail again.

149 " 'we gazed at the island on our farewell' ":

In his journal Steller described his last sight of the foxes as he sailed away from Bering Island:

> We saw the foxes on the beach inspect our dwellings with the greatest glee and occupy them as theirs; it seemed to amaze them that no one hindered them as usual. Besides, they found so many remnants of fat and meat come to them as their share in one fell swoop, to which diversion we left them on our part from the bottom of our hearts.

149 "'the property which we had left behind'":

When the Admiralty learned of Captain Commander Bering's death, they notified his widow, Anna, in St. Petersburg. Waxell sent her Bering's sword, silver shoe buckles, and gold watch. Anna wrote a touching letter to the naval officials in Kamchatka, asking them to also send Bering's nightcap of blue satin with gold embroidery. Unfortunately, the cap had already been sold with the rest of Bering's possessions in Kamchatka at an auction held by Captain Spangberg, who purchased many items himself. It was the standard practice in the Russian Navy for a deceased officer's most valuable possessions to be returned to his widow with all other items to be sold to the highest bidder. The revenue from Bering's auction went to Anna.

151 "Everyone was ill by the time":

Captain Chirikov spent the last two weeks of his voyage in his cabin, bedridden with scurvy. His only healthy officer, the navigator Ivan Yelagin, steered the *St. Paul* back to Avacha Bay, arriving on October 10, 1740. Chirikov was generous in praise of his navigator and raised him to the rank of fleet lieutenant in gratitude for his service.

The captain only gradually regained his health. He was able to send off the report of his voyage to the Senate on December 7, three days before Bering died on Bering Island. When the *St. Peter* did not return, Chirikov planned a search party. On May 25, 1741, as soon as the ice broke up, it left Avacha Bay in the *St. Paul*. After a month at sea the party gave up the search and returned to Okhotsk. Chirikov served as supreme commander of the expedition until he returned to St. Petersburg in 1746, leaving the last of the expeditionary forces in Waxell's hands in Yeniseisk. The Senate had officially ended the Second Kamchatka Expedition on September 25, 1743. In 1747, Chirikov was appointed director of the Naval Academy and raised to the rank of captain commander. Aleksei Chirikov died of tuberculosis and the residual effects of scurvy in St. Petersburg the following year.

Sven Waxell was the only man to serve on the two Kamchatka expeditions from beginning to end. When he finally reached St. Petersburg with Khitrov in 1749, they corrected and completed the charts from the expedition together. Both men became captains in that year. In 1756,

Waxell finished writing his account of the expedition. When he died in 1762, his son Laurentz was already a captain in the Russian Navy. Waxell's account was used by Professor Müller and Russian historians until it was lost sometime after 1851. The manuscript, rediscovered in a bookshop in St. Petersburg (at that time Leningrad) in 1938, was soon published.

In 1753, Safron Khitrov became a rear admiral. Three years later he died, having attained the highest rank of any member of the expedition.

151 "a letter and a parcel from Brigitta Helena":

Waiting for Steller in Bolsheretsk was a letter from his wife with a copy of *Flora Lapponica* by Carolus Linnaeus. Steller learned the sad news that his dear friend at the Academy the botanist Professor Amman, with whom he had spent many happy days in the field, had died in St. Petersburg. On his deathbed, the botanist had directed that his copy of *Flora Lapponica*, the result of the scientific journey taken by Linnaeus to Lapland in 1732, should be sent to Steller in Kamchatka. Steller wrote to his wife asking that she buy and send to him all the works of Linnaeus.

Carolus Linnaeus (1707–78) was a Swedish naturalist who established systems of scientific nomenclature and scientific classification. Although there was some prudish resistance to his system of classification due to its sexual nature (Linnaeus described a plant as having "many wives" or "many husbands" if it had more than one pistil or stamen), so that one British naturalist complained of his "nomenclatural wantonness," the Linnaean system was soon accepted throughout the European scientific community. After Linnaeus defined his "sexual system," the classification of plants and animals changed, responding to the need to recognize affinities beyond the sexual. This new arrangement is called the "natural system" and was introduced by Antoine-Laurent de Jussieu (1748–1836) in his book *Genera Plantarum* in 1789. Linnaeus's scientific nomenclature, however, has endured and forms the basis of the system we still use today, with its kingdoms, classes, orders, genera, and species. As an eighteenth-century scientist, Linnaeus used Latin instead of English or his native language, Swedish. That is why we are *Homo sapiens* and not "Intellectual Man."

The binomial or trinomial (that is, two- or three-part) Latin name given by the first person to publish (in the proper way) a description of a plant or animal is now considered its accepted scientific name. Unfortunately for Steller's reputation, his descriptions remained in manuscript, and the Linnaean naming system was not fully established until ten years after his death, with the publication of Linnaeus's *Species Plantarum* for botanical (plant) names in 1753 and the 10th edition of his *Systema Naturae* for zoological (animal) names in 1758. As a result, none of the plants and animals that Steller was the first to collect and describe bear his name as author. His name does, however, appear as an epithet in the descriptions of his discoveries eventually published by other naturalists: these may be recognized by such terms as *stelleri, stelleris,* or *stelleriana.*

152 "whale hunting ceremony and then the whale hunt":
    Steller wrote a detailed account of the whale hunt of the Olyutor Koriaks, which began with the symbolic pursuit of a wooden whale. He admired the ingenious means the tribe had found to make use of every part of the animal.

> All the inhabitants' households on Kamchatka greatly benefit from the whales. They make the skin into leather, especially for shoe soles and thongs. They eat the fat and meat and burn the oil as fuel. They use both baleen and ribs to construct their *baidaras* [boats] and to make fishnets, fox traps, and water buckets. They make sled runners, knife handles, and all kinds of rings and snaps for their dog harnesses from the two bones of the lower jaw, and from the intestines all kinds of floats and containers in which to keep liquids. From the sinews they make the elastic strings for their fox traps; they also use these sinews in place of twine, for tying all kinds of things requiring strength to hold together. They make mortars from the vertebrae. The cheeks or jaws are gristly and gelatinous and taste quite good, as does the tongue. Flukes and flippers are the next best parts. The blubber is eaten with great gusto during the butchering.

17. Steller on Trial

156 "Johann Georg Gmelin":

After returning to St. Petersburg in 1743, Professor Gmelin spent the next four years preparing for publication his four-volume *Flora Sibirica*, based on Steller's plant collections and his own. The Russian government continued to be very secretive about information gathered on the expedition, doing whatever possible to prevent publication of maps and journals. On the pretense of going to visit his family in Tübingen, Gmelin left St. Petersburg, his fellow professor Müller posting a bond to guarantee his return. Müller lost his money when Gmelin accepted a professorship in botany and chemistry at the University of Tübingen. Gmelin further enraged the authorities in St. Petersburg by breaking his four-year contract as a professor at the Academy and publishing his Siberian diaries in four volumes between 1751 and 1752. The book was highly critical of Russian rule in Siberia. Gmelin received threatening letters from the Academy and warnings from friends that the arm of the Empress reached a long way. He never returned to St. Petersburg, and died in 1755 at the age of forty-six. At the time of his death, there were rumors that he had been poisoned by Russian agents.

160 "A visiting Lutheran minister":

There were so few Protestants in Siberia in the mid-eighteenth century that only a few Lutheran pastors, among them the house chaplain of Governor Lange, Anton Heinrich Königshaven, served the entire region. Königshaven and Steller had probably met in the Archbishop's palace in Irkutsk, or perhaps, being only one year apart in age, at university when studying theology in Wittenberg.

At the time of Steller's death the minister was on an official journey, visiting the small communities of Lutherans scattered throughout the territory of Irkutsk. In this vast land, Steller's death and the minister's visit happened to coincide in Tyumen.

161 "Peter Simon Pallas":

Peter Simon Pallas (1741–1811), a German naturalist and professor at the Academy of Sciences in St. Petersburg, led the Academy Expedition from 1768 to 1774 under the patronage of Catherine II. The Empress welcomed foreign interest in Russia and encouraged publication of documents relating to the Second Kamchatka Expedition and the Academy Expedition. When Pallas returned to St. Petersburg, his works concerning the peoples, flora, and fauna of western Siberia were published in German, English, French, and Russian editions. Pallas used Steller's writings in his own books about Siberia, especially *Flora Rossica*.

Afterword

163 "word of the naturalist's death":

Soon after receiving official word of Steller's death, Brigitta Helena Steller married a tutor of the pageboys at the imperial court. She was almost forty years old at the time; Steller had been away for nine years.

165 "his journals and letters are being carefully transcribed":

Steller's History of Kamchatka became available in Margritt Engel and Karen Willmore's excellent English translation for the first time only in 2003. It covers everything from torturous Kamchadal rites of friendship, which Steller compares to German university hazing rituals, to the use of dried salmon roe as pacifiers for children, with carefully observed descriptions of plants and animals in between. Although it is a scientific account, Steller's personality is revealed in his occasional judgments and asides.

Steller's journal from the *St. Peter* has been published twice in English translation, by Leonhard Stejneger in 1925 and by Margritt Engel and Orcutt W. Frost in 1988. Steller displays a less agreeable side of his character when stuck on a ship with sailors unwilling to take his advice than when traveling independently among the Kamchadals. However, he was undoubtedly the only man on board the *St. Peter* who was in a position to say at the end of the voyage, "I would not exchange the knowledge of nature which I gained on this rotten voyage for great wealth."

SOURCE NOTES

ABBREVIATIONS USED IN THE SOURCE NOTES

Engel & Frost	Georg Wilhelm Steller, *Journal of a Voyage with Bering, 1741–1742*, trans. Margritt Engel and Orcutt W. Frost
Engel & Willmore	Georg Wilhelm Steller, *Steller's History of Kamchatka*, trans. Margritt Engel and Karen Willmore
Fjodorova et al.	Tatjana Fjodorova, Birgit Leick Lampe, Sigurd Rambusch, and Tage Sørensen, *Martin Spangsberg*
Golder I	F. A. Golder, *Bering's Voyages*, trans. Leonhard Stejneger, Vol. I
Golder II	F. A. Golder, *Bering's Voyages*, trans. Leonhard Stejneger, Vol. II
Jordan	David Starr Jordan, *The Fur Seals and Fur-Seal Islands of the North Pacific Ocean*, Pt. 3 (containing part of Steller's *De Bestiis Marinis*)
Müller	Gerhard Friedrich Müller, *Bering's Voyages*
Stejneger	Leonhard Stejneger, *Georg Wilhelm Steller, the Pioneer of Alaskan Natural History*
Waxell	Sven Waxell, *The American Expedition*, trans. M. A. Michael

1. *Sonntagskind*: A Sunday's Child

7 "I am shortly going to fall . . . You will unexpectedly make": Stejneger, 44.

2. Russia's Great Explorations: The First and Second Kamchatka Expeditions

18 "The whole undertaking was planned": Stejneger, 97.

3. On to Russia: Stöller Becomes Steller

26 "While the good Steller": Stejneger, 68.

27 "a lively, wild woman": Stejneger, 83.

4. Steller's Journey Begins

34–36 "We saw that our ship . . . The next day we found nothing": Stepan P. Krasheninnikov, *Explorations of Kamchatka, North Pacific Scimitar*, 352–53.

39 "He was not troubled about his clothing": Stejneger, 146, 148.

40 "passionately in love with science": Stejneger, 147.

41 "I have compared the muscles": Stejneger, 163.

41 "I have entirely forgotten her": Stejneger, 135.

5. The Barguzin Mountains

43–44 "The view fairly overwhelmed me": Stejneger, 168.

44–45 "When a tame roebuck": Ian Jackson's translation of Peter Simon Pallas, *Flora Rossica* (1784–88), Vol. I, Pt. 1, 45.

45 "Beginning of a Russian": Stejneger, 171.

46 "they can be drawn": Stejneger, 169.

7. Captain Martin Spangberg: Okhotsk, the Kuril Islands, and Japan

56 "the sea mist is thick": Fjodorova et al., 136.

57–58 "The boats have decks . . . These Japanese are middle and small-sized": Fjodorova et al., 151.

58–59 "Their faces are like those": Fjodorova et al., 156.

59 "Their clothes seemed to be made of wool": Fjodorova et al., 172.

59 "There was an iron pipe": Fjodorova et al., 167.

59–60 "The sailors looked like Dutchmen": Fjodorova et al., 166–67.

60 "to search for new lands": Müller, 34.

8. The Volcanic Wilderness of Kamchatka

67 "The sleds are engineered": Engel & Willmore, 279, 97–98.

68 "They imitate Captain Spangberg": Engel & Willmore, 255.

68 "Whoever comes to Kamchatka": Engel & Willmore, 218.

69 "A small number of these people": Golder I, 17.

69–71 "They liked to settle": Engel & Willmore, 162–64, 164–66.

71–72 "The horned puffin . . . The tufted puffin": Engel & Willmore, 135.

72–73 "The old squaw": Engel & Willmore, 140.

74 "On Kamchatka the snow reflects": Engel & Willmore, 43.

74 "Along the ocean a tall grass": Engel & Willmore, 58–59.

75–76 "Out of *gramine Cyperoide*": Engel & Willmore, 59–60.

76 "All of these bulbs": Engel & Willmore, 65.

76–77 "They take part of this supply": Engel & Willmore, 65.

77–78 "Scurvy actually bothers": Engel & Willmore, 47.

78 "They . . . know the efficacy": Engel & Willmore, 58.

78 "I eagerly took pains": Golder II, 99.

9. Avacha Bay: Steller Signs On to the *St. Peter*

81 "People talk much": Golder II, 100.

10. They Set Sail for America

87 "No matter what we observed": Golder II, 26.

88 "It can easily be imagined": Golder II, 34.

88 "It was one of his favourite sayings": Waxell, 65.

89 "Only on one point were all unanimous": Golder II, 37.

89 "When I asked to be sent off": Engel & Frost, 64.

90–91 "On my departure from the ship": Engel & Frost, 65–66.

92 "Dead tired, I made in the meantime": Golder II, 50.

93–94 "As evening was already nearing": Golder II, 59–60.

94–95 "An iron kettle": Golder II, 51–52, 53–54.

96 "Two hours before daybreak": Golder II, 60–61.

96 "The time here spent": Golder II, 53–54.

11. Return Voyage: Kayaks and Death

99 "Continuous stormy and wet weather": Golder II, 61, 63–64, 74.

100 "I was scarcely ashore": Engel & Frost, 89.

101 "Why, what is the matter": Golder II, 78.

101 "[We] found here": Golder II, 84–85.

102 "On this day we buried": Golder II, 87.

103 "Towards evening, we were hurriedly called": Golder II, 86.

103 "and at the first attempt": Golder II, 89.

104 "The *Lapathum* I prescribed": Engel & Frost, 94.

105–106 "We had scarcely dropped": Golder II, 90–92.

106 "I could see that they were afraid": Waxell, 114.

106–107 "After a short consultation": Golder II, 93–94.

107 "He was evidently the eldest": Waxell, 115.

108 "Although I advised": Golder II, 94–95.

109–10 "I counted nine islanders on the beach": Golder II, 96, 104, 95–96.

12. A Devastating Voyage: Scurvy and Williwaws

111–12 "The unwholesome water": Golder II, 106, 86.

112 "I have such pains": Golder I, 200.

113 "We again had a very violent storm": Golder II, 115.

113–14 "About five o'clock in the morning": Golder II, 115–16.

114 "When we had scarcely more": Golder II, 85.

115 "Misery and death": Golder II, 121.

115 "To our great astonishment": Golder II, 129.

116 " 'Get out, hold your tongue' ": Golder II, 133–34.

116 "At last . . . my turn came": Golder II, 134.

117 "It was now already night": Golder II, 135.

117 "One asked, 'Is the water' ": Engel & Frost, 126.

117 "Ovtsin and the boatswain": Golder II, 136.

13. Kamchatka or a Barren Island?

118 "God knows whether this is Kamchatka!": Golder II, 137.

119 "our 'grave' ": Engel & Frost, 131.

119 "We all realized that rank": Golder II, 148, 141–42.

120–21 "The foxes, which now turned up": Engel & Frost, 134.

121 "This animal . . . far surpasses": Golder II, 209.

122 "More sick [men] were brought ashore": Golder 142–44.

123 "such as axes, knives": Golder II, 148.

123–24 "While thus taking upon myself": Golder II, 150–51.

124 "They could not lose heart": Müller, 115.

124 "We had only a three months' supply": Golder II, 163, note 388.

124 "All the water": Golder II, 209.

125 "Finally Waxell himself": Golder II, 152.

126 "All the sick were finally brought": Engel & Frost, 135.

127 "We were in daily fear": Golder II, 152.

128 "He would undoubtedly": Golder II, 157; 158, note 370.

14. Bering Island

129 "Ivanov and his party": Golder I, 233.

129 "After the death of our leader": Golder II, 159, 160.

130 "Everyone knew at all times": Golder II, 167.

130–31 "Sea-otter flesh": Waxell, 137–38.

131–32 "What contributed to our wretchedness": Waxell, 138–40.

133 "He said that if I would give him": Waxell, 147–48.

134 "Everything was taken out": Golder II, 176.

134 "The pleasant spring weather": Golder II, 178.

135 "As soon as the snow": Waxell, 142.

135 "1. Kamchatkan sweet grass": Golder II, 178, note 425.

15. Sea Eagles and Sea Cows: The Natural History of Bering Island

137–38 "In June they give birth": Golder II, 213.

138 "It makes its nest of brush": Engel & Willmore, 145.

139 "From the ring around the eyes . . . the flesh of one": Errol Fuller, *Extinct Birds*, 40.

140 "Every day for ten months": Stejneger, 354.

140 "They masticate differently": Jordan, 186.

140 "These gluttonous animals": Stejneger, 355.

141 "The animal has no hair": Jordan, 197.

141 "When the tide came in": Jordan, 197, 183, 197–98.

142–43 "Birds and fishes migrate": Jordan, 202, 205, 206.

144–45 "I lived a season": Jordan, 209, 208, 209, 208, 209, 210.

145–46 "As to the beauty of the animal": Jordan, 215, 216–17.

16. A Safe Return to Kamchatka

147–48 "It came to pass": Golder II, 181, note 433.

148–49 "All left their huts . . . In the morning": Golder II, 182–83, 159 and note 276, 183.

149 "This afternoon we spent": Engel & Frost, 167.

149 "Early on Tuesday, the 17th": Golder II, 185–86, 186–87.

150 "Agai! Agai!": Stejneger, 377.

151 "My soul is fired": Stejneger, 168.

152 "If you ask them the meaning": Stejneger, 418.

153–54 "An overreaching and misunderstood order": Stejneger, 395.

154 "Kamchadal arch conspirators": Stejneger, 425.

17. Steller on Trial

157–58 "This sudden separation": Stejneger, 475–76.

159 "was over in eight days": Stejneger, 484.

Afterword

164 "I lament": Stejneger, 489.

Notes

178 "(1) to find out for certain": Müller, 34.

180 "My Bering had absolutely no idea": Peter Ulf Møller and Natasha Okhotina Lind, *Under Vitus Bering's Command*, 243.

181 "Much that in other places": Stejneger, 70.

185 "We stopped at a *zimovye*": Stejneger, 145.

187 "The shaman sat": Piers Vitebsky, *The Reindeer People*, 387.

189 "my Cossack": Golder II, 14.

190 "In a nutshell, this is the best harbour": Waxell, 96.

192–93 "I think it would be only reasonable": Waxell, 103.

194 "In 1790, when the Billings expedition": Golder I, 98, note 38.

195 "oranges and lemons": C. P. Stewart and Douglas Guthrie, eds., *Lind's Treatise on Scurvy* (Edinburgh: Edinburgh University Press, 1953), 148.

196 "When the crew of the yawl": Waxell, 111–12.

199 "We saw the foxes on the beach": Engel & Frost, 167.

202 "All the inhabitants' households": Engel & Willmore, 78–79.

204 "I would not exchange": Stejneger, 390.

BIBLIOGRAPHY

Bancroft, Hubert Howe. *History of Alaska*. San Francisco: A. L. Bancroft & Co., 1886. Bancroft was neither a man of letters nor a scholar, but his massive compilations contain valuable source material.

Black, J. L. *G.-F. Müller and the Imperial Russian Academy*. Kingston: McGill-Queen's University Press, 1986. An excellent account of Professor Gerhard Friedrich Müller's career and the complicated history of Russia's Imperial Academy of Sciences.

Blunt, Wilfrid. *The Compleat Naturalist: A Life of Linnaeus*. London: Collins, 1971. This is the most literate life of Linnaeus in English. Steller was very interested in the system being developed by Linnaeus to classify plants and animals. In a letter, he asked his wife to send any new books by Linnaeus to him in Siberia. After the naturalist's death, Linnaeus secretly obtained sixty-two packets of seeds from Steller's American and Siberian plants directly from the Demidov greenhouses, circumventing the Senate's restrictions on expedition discoveries.

Buberl, Brigitte, and Michael Dückershoff, eds. *Palast des Wissens: Die Kunst und Wunderkammer Zar Peters des Großen*. 2 vol. Munich: Hirmer Verlag, 2003. A beautifully illustrated German exhibition catalog of objects from Peter the Great's magnificent cabinet of curiosities, with essays by different scholars, sometimes contradictory, describing the political, scientific, and historical significance of Peter's collection.

Carpenter, Kenneth J. *The History of Scurvy and Vitamin C*. Cambridge, U.K.: Cambridge University Press, 1986. The best modern history of scurvy. The author carefully evaluates the contributions of men from many nations and describes outbreaks of scurvy into the twentieth century.

Chekhov, Anton. *A Journey to Sakhalin*. Trans. Brian Reeve. Cambridge, U.K.: Ian Faulkner, 1993. Chekhov traveled in his own carriage, using post-horses, through Siberia to the prison island of Sakhalin. This is a most engaging account of travel across Siberia in the 1890s, 150 years after Steller.

Divin, Vasilii A. *The Great Russian Navigator A. I. Chirikov*. Trans. and annotated by Raymond H. Fisher. Fairbanks: University of Alaska Press, 1993. This is a thorough account of Chirikov's life. However, the translator explains in his foreword that the book was written during the Communist era and is deeply tainted by the political need to make all the Russians on the expedition, including Khitrov, look superior to the foreigners involved. Divin quotes Chirikov's scathing opinion of Spangberg, pages 102, 103, and elsewhere.

Fjodorova, Tatjana; Birgit Leick Lampe; Sigurd Rambusch; and Tage Sørensen. *Martin Spangsberg; A Danish Explorer in Russian Service*. Esbjerg: Fiskeri- og Søfartsmuseet, 1999. The authors, both Russian and Danish, drawing on recently discovered archival material, present for the first time a balanced view of the character and conduct of the upper echelons of the expedition's personnel.

Frost, Orcutt W. *Bering: The Russian Discovery of America*. New Haven, Conn.: Yale University Press, 2003. This is a highly readable life of Captain Commander Bering, although Frost's interpretation of Anna Bering's character is based on his mistranslation of a passage in one of her letters. Orcutt Frost sees Steller's Pietist Lutheran beliefs as the key to his character and actions.

Fuller, Errol. *Extinct Birds*. London: Viking/Rainbird, 1987. Reproduces an image and description of the spectacled cormorant.

Giroud, Vincent. *St. Petersburg: A Portrait of a Great City*. New Haven, Conn.: Beinecke Rare Book & Manuscript Library, 2003. This catalog was produced by Yale to commemorate the three hundredth anniversary of the founding of St. Petersburg. The introductory essays and detailed, informative captions to the many illustrations follow the history of St. Petersburg from the time of Peter the Great to the end of czarist Russia, when St. Petersburg was renamed Leningrad.

Golder, F. A. *Bering's Voyages: An Account of the Efforts of the Russians to Determine the Relation of Asia and America*. Trans. and in part annotated by Leonhard Stejneger. 2 vols. New York: American Geographical Society, 1922–25. The first English translation, with excellent notes, of Steller's journal and the logbooks from the voyage of the *St. Peter*.

Stejneger made this translation based upon printed texts from 1781 and 1793, edited by the great naturalist Peter Simon Pallas. I have chosen to use some passages from this translation and others from Margritt Engel and Orcutt W. Frost's more recent translation. These two translations are my primary sources for information about Steller's voyage to Alaska.

Hayes, Derek. *Historical Atlas of the Pacific Northwest.* Seattle: Sasquatch Books, 1999. This is a compilation of early printed and manuscript maps with notes and short essays about the mapmakers and the locations depicted. It includes some of the maps from the two Kamchatka expeditions.

Hintzsche, Wieland, and Thomas Nickol, eds. *Die Große Nordische Expedition: Georg Wilhelm Steller (1709–1746), ein Lutheraner erforscht Sibirien und Alaska.* Gotha: Justus Perthes Verlag, 1996. Descriptions and many illustrations of different aspects of Steller's life and travels. Page 237 contains an account of the present-day influence of Steller's writings on the revival of Kamchadal customs and ceremonies.

Jordan, David Starr. *The Fur Seals and Fur-Seal Islands of the North Pacific Ocean.* Pt. 3. Washington, D.C.: Government Printing Office, 1899. This volume contains the first English translation, by Walter and Jennie Emerson Miller, of part of Steller's *De Bestiis Marinis.*

Krasheninnikov, Stepan P. *Explorations of Kamchatka, North Pacific Scimitar. Report of a Journey Made to Explore Eastern Siberia in 1735–1741, by Order of the Russian Imperial Government.* Trans. with intro. and notes by A. P. Crownhart-Vaughan. Portland: Oregon Historical Society, 1972. This is the first complete translation of Krasheninnikov's classic work on Kamchatka based upon the notes he made during his three years on the peninsula as well as Steller's manuscripts. Krasheninnikov does not always give proper credit to Steller for his contributions. While full of information, his writings lack the poetry, the beautiful analogies, and the comparisons that we find in Steller's descriptions of Kamchatka.

Møller, Peter Ulf, and Natasha Okhotina Lind, eds. *Under Vitus Bering's Command: New Perspectives on the Russian Kamchatka Expeditions.* Aarhus: Aarhus University Press, 2003. This is a collection of articles in Russian and English covering everything from the slanderous attacks on Bering as he prepared for the next step of the expedition in Yakutsk to his wife's clavichord. Professor Carol Urness describes the importance of mapping on the First Kamchatka Expedition and the way historians, from Müller onward, have confused the true purpose and accomplishments of that expedition. The Bering letters from Okhotsk, recently discovered unopened in Moscow, are translated into English and annotated for the first time in this volume.

Müller, Gerhard Friedrich. *Bering's Voyages: The Reports from Russia*. Trans., with commentary, by Carol Urness. Fairbanks: University of Alaska Press, 1986. This is the definitive translation of the account by Müller, the historian of the expedition, with the translator's comprehensive introduction to Russian exploration and Müller's life and times. Waxell's account was the chief source for Müller, although Steller's journal was also used. Müller accentuates Steller's importance as minister and doctor on the voyage.

Müller-Bahlke, Thomas. *The Cabinet of Artefacts and Curiosities in the Francke Foundations in Halle*. Halle: Franckesche Stiftungen zu Halle, 2004. A brief history of the Francke Foundations with photographs and descriptions of the contents of each of the decorated cases in the recently restored cabinet of curiosities.

———. *Die Wunderkammer: Die Kunst- und Naturalienkammer der Franckeschen Stiftungen zu Halle (Saale)*. Halle: Verlag der Franckeschen Stiftungen, 1998. A history of the Francke Foundations' Cabinet of Artifacts and Curiosities with an account of its recent restoration and many large color illustrations of the cabinets and their contents.

Nigge, Klaus. "The Russian Realm of Steller's Sea-Eagles." *National Geographic*, March 1999, pp. 61–71. Dramatic close-up photographs of the world's most impressive eagle, making one wonder at Steller's curiosity and sangfroid when he climbed up to a nest.

Posselt, Doris, ed. *Die Große Nordische Expedition von 1733 bis 1743: Aus Berichten der Forschungsreisenden Johann Georg Gmelin und Georg Wilhelm Steller*. Munich: Verlag C. H. Beck, 1990. A modern German reprint of Gmelin's *Travels in Siberia* and Steller's *History of Kamchatka* with notes and illustrations.

Röhrich, Lutz. *Das große Lexikon der sprichwörtlichen Redensarten*. 3 vols. Freiburg im Breisgau: Herder, 1991. This vast compendium of German proverbial phraseology contains information about the *Sonn-tagskind* on p. 1492.

Ryan, W. F. *The Bathhouse at Midnight: An Historical Survey of Magic and Divination in Russia.* University Park, Pa.: Pennsylvania State University Press, 1999. The first general study of a fascinating field, covering everything from amulets to Yuletide divination in Russia.

Stejneger, Leonhard. *Georg Wilhelm Steller, the Pioneer of Alaskan Natural History.* Cambridge, Mass.: Harvard University Press, 1936. I owe my greatest debt to this wonderful book, written over a period of fifty years by a man as fascinated by nature as Steller himself. In 1882, Stejneger was commissioned to collect a sea cow skeleton—that is, the bones of an animal which had been extinct for a hundred years—on Bering Island, its only known habitat, where Steller had carefully observed it. Stejneger spent eighteen months on the island tracing Steller's footsteps. He pieced together two skeletons for the National Museum of Natural History in Washington, D.C., and the Museum of Comparative Zoology at Harvard University, where they are still on display. Stejneger spent the rest of his life assembling the scattered facts and dispelling the false rumors concerning Steller and his historical period. He translated Steller's journal on the *St. Peter* and traveled to Kayak Island. Steller's biography was perhaps too specialized to reach a wide audience and is a rare book outside of libraries today. Even the British reprint of 1970 has long been out of print.

Steller, Georg Wilhelm. *Briefe und Dokumente 1740.* ed. Wieland Hintzsche, Thomas Nickol, and Olga Vladimirovna Novochatko. Halle: Verlag der Franckeschen Stiftungen, 2000. Steller's letters and documents sent to the Academy or to other members of the expedition from Siberia in 1740 were discovered by Professor Hintzsche in the archives in St. Petersburg and meticulously edited for this volume.

————. *Journal of a Voyage with Bering, 1741–1742.* Trans. Margritt Engel and Orcutt W. Frost. Stanford, Calif.: Stanford University Press, 1988. The second English translation of Steller's journal, this time from a manuscript discovered after the completion of Stejneger's 1925 translation of the Pallas 1793 edition.

————. *Steller's History of Kamchatka: Collected Information Concerning the*

History of Kamchatka, Its Peoples, Their Manners, Names, Lifestyles, and Various Customary Practices. Ed. Marvin W. Falk. Trans. Margritt Engel and Karen Willmore. Fairbanks: University of Alaska Press, 2003. Professor Margritt Engel made the preliminary translation of Steller's journal for Orcutt W. Frost in 1988 and spent ten years with Karen Willmore translating Steller's book about Kamchatka. The book contains some graphic descriptions (including courtship rituals, sexual practices, and hallucinogenic mushrooms) and beautifully written passages about nature, creation myths, practical uses of natural materials, and hunting techniques, with all sorts of miscellaneous information.

Vitebsky, Piers. *The Reindeer People: Living with Animals and Spirits in Siberia.* Boston: Houghton Mifflin Company, 2005. For twenty years the author made annual visits to a small community of Eveny reindeer herders in northeastern Siberia, three hundred miles northwest of Yakutsk. His study is a deep personal appreciation of the culture and history of these nomadic people.

Waxell, Sven. *The American Expedition.* Trans. M. A. Michael. London: William Hodge and Co., 1952. This is a most engaging and personal account of the Second Kamchatka Expedition written by Bering's second-in-command. The Russian Naval Academy had been known to exile and execute officers who had not done their duty. By comparing Waxell's account with Steller's private journal, one can see at which moments on the voyage Waxell stretched or hid the truth so as to protect himself and his friends, particularly Khitrov, from censure or worse. The introduction to this English version, however, repeats false rumors about Steller.

Gerhard Müller used Waxell's writings extensively in his report to the Senate. The original German manuscript then disappeared and did not come to light again until 1938. In 1940, it was translated into Russian, and then from Russian into Danish. The Danish text was later turned into this English version, and then translated back again into German, the original in Leningrad now being inaccessible to Western scholars. Working from the original manuscript in St. Petersburg and another since discovered in Moscow, Wieland Hintzsche is preparing a definitive edition of Waxell's original German text.

INDEX